MAMMALS

OF BRITAIN & EUROPE

Key to coloured tabs

The mammals in this book are arranged in systematic order, according to their classification. Similar species are grouped into genera, the similar genera into families, and the families are arranged within the orders listed below. Each order is given a colour reference marker. Use this coloured square at the corner of the pages to help you find the different groups of mammals as you flick through the book.

Hedgehogs, Moles and Shrews

Bats

Rabbits and Hares

Rodents

Primates

Carnivores

Seals

Hoofed Mammals

Whales and Dolphins

KINGFISHER FIELD GUIDES

MAMMALS
OF BRITAIN & EUROPE

Written by
JOHN A. BURTON

KING*f*ISHER

KINGFISHER
Kingfisher Publications Plc
New Penderel House
283–288 High Holborn
London WC1V 7HZ
www.kingfisherpub.com

First published by Kingfisher Publications Plc in 1991
This edition first published in 2002

10 9 8 7 6 5 4 3 2 1
1TR/0104/PP/U*UNI/135MA

A CIP catalogue record for this book
is available from the British Library

ISBN 0-86272-692-1

Senior Editor: Stuart Cooper
Assistant Editor: Andrea Moran

Illustrations: William Oliver pp. 9, 11, 18–19, 24, 111–188, cover
Guy Troughton pp. 8, 10, 12–17, 28–110, cover

Colour separations by Newsele Litho SpA, Milan
Printed in Portugal

CONTENTS

INTRODUCTION

The mammals are a remarkably diverse group. They range from shrews the size of a bumble bee to the Blue Whale, which weighs almost 200 tonnes. They also vary greatly in structure, having adapted to many different ways of life. Bats have wings for flight and live a nocturnal existence using echolocation. Moles have powerful forepaws for digging the extensive burrows in which they spend almost all their lives. Whales and dolphins have fins and other adaptations for an entirely aquatic existence.

Some mammals are remarkably easy to identify, while many species need to be examined closely in order to be positively identified. Unlike birds, which can often be identified by their distinctive plumage, many small mammals look identical, and there are frequently several colour variants within a species. Their diagnostic characters are often small differences in tooth structure, relative measurements, or DNA.

Using descriptions, fact panels and illustrations, this book provides a basic identification guide to the mammals of Britain and Europe, and aims to stimulate an interest in mammals and their conservation. Emphasis has been placed on those species that are most abundant, and that the keen naturalist can reasonably expect to identify in the field. For the more obscure species, specialist guide books will be needed, such as the selection listed on page 192.

Mammal names

Most European mammals have an English or common name, for example Wood Mouse, and a scientific name, in this case *Apodemus sylvaticus*. The latter consists of two parts, the generic name (*Apodemus*), and the specific name (*sylvaticus*). These names are usually italicized, and the generic name is always written with an initial capital. Closely related species share the same generic name – jackals, wolves and dogs are all in the genus *Canis*. Scientific names are based on Latin, though often very crudely, and a translation of them will generally describe the animal concerned. For instance, *Mus* is Latin for mouse, and *domesticus* means that it is found around human habitations. Sometimes a third name is added, to denote a subspecies – a geographically distinct population or 'race'. These finer distinctions are not described in this book.

The scientific nomenclature of most European mammals is fairly standardized, but you will find some variation between different guide books. This is because new species are being discovered and others are reclassified as further details of their structure and distribution are uncovered. Particularly affected are bats, shrews and small rodents. An equals sign is used to denote alternative names which may be used. Many of the common names for mammals are rarely used, particularly those of the lesser known shrews and voles, so it is worth trying to become familiar with their scientific names.

SCOPE OF THIS BOOK

The area covered by this guide extends from Scandinavia and northern Russia in the north, down to the islands of the Mediterranean in the south; from the Atlantic coast in the west to the Ural mountains, Black Sea, Caspian Sea and the Aegean Islands in the east. (For the purposes of this book, Europe is considered as extending west from the Crimea, and the area excluded from the range maps is shaded grey.)

Range and distribution

Range maps are a particularly important aid to identifying mammals, since compared with birds, most mammals lack mobility. However, it is also important to be aware that even within an area marked on a map, the population density will vary enormously. A species will not be found in all parts of its range, but only in suitable habitats. Details of distribution are incomplete for many European mammals, and observations of even some of the more common species (particularly around the edge of their range) are likely to be of interest and value. Hence ? in some areas. Readers are encouraged to note their observations and send any that might be of interest to one of the appropriate organizations listed on page 192, or to the author (c/o the publishers).

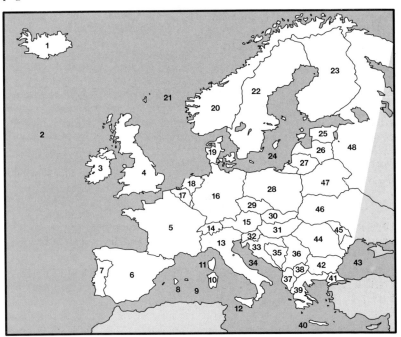

1 Iceland 2 Atlantic Ocean 3 Ireland 4 Britain 5 France 6 Spain 7 Portugal 8 Balearic Islands
9 Mediterranean Sea 10 Sardinia 11 Corsica 12 Sicily 13 Italy 14 Switzerland 15 Austria 16 Germany
17 Belgium 18 Holland 19 Denmark 20 Norway 21 Norwegian Sea 22 Sweden 23 Finland 24 Baltic Sea
25 Estonia 26 Latvia 27 Lithuania 28 Poland 29 Czech Republic 30 Slovakia 31 Hungary 32 Slovenia
33 Croatia 34 Adriatic Sea 35 Bosnia & Herzegovina 36 Yugoslavia 37 Albania 38 Macedonia 39 Greece
40 Crete 41 Turkey 42 Bulgaria 43 Black Sea 44 Romania 45 Moldova 46 Ukraine 47 Belarus 48 Russia

Introduction

HOW TO USE THIS BOOK

Because mammals are so diverse it is important first of all to familiarize yourself with the main groups. By reading the descriptions on pages 9–10, and using the colour key on the second page of this book, you will soon learn what these groups are, as well as their main features. It is not too difficult to distinguish a shrew from a mouse or a bat, but within a group it is important to know which features are likely to be diagnostic.

Once you are familiar with the main groups it is then possible to try to match any animal you have seen against the illustrations. Having found the illustration that most closely resembles the animal, first check the distribution map and see if the species is likely to occur in the area you are in. Then read the text carefully, to see if the description fits, and check the details given in the fact panel. If the animal you think you have spotted does not occur in that particular location, check the distribution maps and descriptions of all similar species mentioned in the same section. A good rule of thumb for a beginner is that you are most likely to see the common species. Do not expect to see rarities. If the description does not fit exactly, make allowances for individual variation. In this guide, all British and most European species have been included.

Annotation around the illustrations highlights important features

A text summarizes the main characteristics of each mammal, and draws attention to important aspects of its behaviour. The range is described as well as any similar species with which it may be confused.

A distribution map shows the range of the species overall. Within this area the frequency of occurrence varies widely.

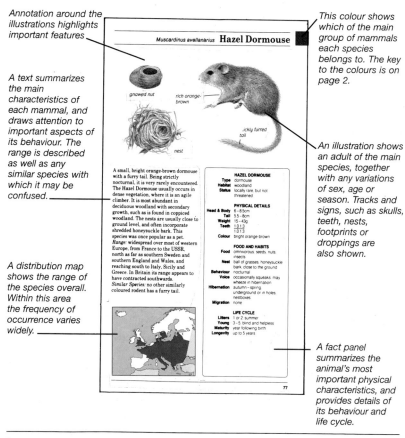

This colour shows which of the main group of mammals each species belongs to. The key to the colours is on page 2.

An illustration shows an adult of the main species, together with any variations of sex, age or season. Tracks and signs, such as skulls, teeth, nests, footprints or droppings are also shown.

A fact panel summarizes the animal's most important physical characteristics, and provides details of its behaviour and life cycle.

Introduction

THE MAIN GROUPS OF MAMMALS

The critical features for identifying species within each group of mammals are dealt with in greater detail on pages 16–19, but first it is important to become familiar with the main groups.

There are two groups of marine mammals: seals (pinnipeds) and whales (cetaceans). The seals lack a dorsal fin, have large eyes and usually have fairly obvious whiskers. The hind feet are developed into flippers, which are used only for swimming. They often 'haul out' of the water onto rocks and beaches. Seals are often very vocal and can be heard barking from some distance. Their breeding sites often have a characteristic pungent smell.

The cetaceans fall into two main groups: the toothed whales (including sperm whales, dolphins and porpoises) and the baleen whales. In the latter the teeth are replaced with horny plates called baleen, which have ragged fringes used to filter plankton (small animals and plants, including crustaceans and small fish) from the sea. Cetaceans never come ashore, but are occasionally stranded on beaches, when they usually die. Whales have a blow-hole on the top of the head, and they lack whiskers. Their eyes, which are smaller than seals', are set well back on the side of the head. Most whales have a dorsal fin.

The hoofed mammals (ungulates) are diverse in size, ranging from deer the size of a spaniel, to the Elk, which is larger than most cattle. The ungulates are divided into two groups, odd-toed (horses and donkeys), and even-toed (cattle, sheep, goats, and deer). They all have relatively long legs, are usually fairly agile, and often have horns. Some species grow their horns continuously (bovids) but others shed them each year and regrow them before the breeding season (cervids). In most horn-bearing ungulates there are marked differences between the sexes. In many species, only the males bear horns; in others, both sexes have horns but males' are larger than females'.

The carnivores are one of the most diverse groups of mammals, including the mouse-sized, slender weasels, the raccoon and mongoose, and the massive bears. Their most distinctive feature is their teeth – the large canines and the carnassial, a large molar which is particularly sharp and capable of cutting flesh. Most carnivores are relatively short-legged and they show considerable colour variation. The majority are predatory, feeding on a wide range of prey animals. However, several species are scavengers, and some feed extensively on vegetable matter at certain times of the year.

The weasel is the smallest European carnivore, and like most other carnivores is an alert and active hunter.

Introduction

Rodents and lagomorphs (rabbits and hares) were at one time classified together, but are no longer thought to be closely related, although their tooth structure is similar. Both have chisel-like front teeth (incisors) followed by a gap (diastema) and a row of flat cheek teeth (molars). The lagomorphs have a second pair of upper incisors behind the first.

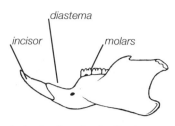

A typical rodent jaw, showing the sharp incisor, followed by a gap (diastema) and a row of ridged molars.

Rodents are not only the most abundant mammals in most parts of Europe, they are also the most diverse. The majority are similar to rats and mice – the most familiar rodents – but the group also includes the Porcupine, the Flying Squirrel and the subterranean mole rats. Rodents feed mostly on seeds and roots, but they nearly all eat some animal matter such as grubs, molluscs and even the young of other small mammals and birds. Rabbits and hares are among the most frequently seen European mammals; they are relatively large, often occur in fairly open habitats and are often active by day. They can be distinguished from other mammals by their long ears and short, fluffy tails. They have powerful hind legs and are capable of short, very fast bursts of speed.

In Europe there are three groups of insectivores: the moles and Desman (an aquatic mole), the hedgehogs, which have fur modified into protective spines, and the shrews, the most generalized of the European insectivores. They are thought to be among the most primitive mammals, due to their simple tooth structure. Most insectivores are relatively small and the most abundant species, the shrews, resemble mice, but they are distinguished by their rows of small, pointed teeth, together with a longish snout and dark, velvety fur. All feed mostly on invertebrates, including earthworms, insect larvae and molluscs, but they will eat almost any animal that is small enough to be devoured, including baby mice, small frogs and other small vertebrates.

Bats, as a group, are the most easily identified mammals – they are the only ones with wings. These are quite unlike the wings of birds, and are formed by a web of skin between four extended fingers and the body. Bats are nocturnal and spend the day hidden in caves, cellars, tree holes and similar places. The different species of bat are among the most difficult to separate, even on close examination.

Some bats hide in crevices when roosting, but Horseshoe Bats hang free from the roofs of caves and cellars.

Introduction

Domestic and feral species, introductions, escapes

When domesticated animals revert to the wild and live in independent, self-perpetuating populations, they are referred to as feral. One of the most common feral mammals in Europe is the Cat, but populations of Feral Dogs, Ferrets and other species occur. The Raccoon and American Mink have been domesticated or semi-domesticated on fur farms, and have subsequently escaped into the wild. Feral mammals are distinct from the wild species they are descended from, although populations may interbreed, such as Polecats and their domesticated descendants, feral Ferrets. Several domesticated mammals are allowed to range in semi-freedom, such as sheep, goats, cattle and horses. However, these animals are not truly feral, as their breeding may be controlled and they may be artificially fed in winter.

Several species have been deliberately introduced into the wild from overseas – the Cottontail, Grey Squirrel and Porcupine are all present in Europe as a result of deliberate introductions. Reintroductions occur when a species has become extinct in one area and survivors are imported from elsewhere. Species which have been translocated and reintroduced include the Wild Boar, Lynx and Beaver. Many countries in Europe now have laws to control or ban the release of mammals into the wild, since many introduced species have proved to be pests.

Finally, there are sporadic escapes of such species as the Guinea Pig and Gerbil, which are not native to Europe, but are widely kept in captivity. They occasionally escape into the wild, sometimes establishing breeding populations. These populations, however, are cyclical, and do not last long enough to be regarded as feral.

Plotting the distribution of escapes and feral species is particularly difficult as it is often very changeable. The distribution maps give an indication of where such species might be encountered, rather than where they have been recorded.

Feral Cats are widespread in Europe, and often interbreed with Wild Cats. Feral animals are usually variable in colour, reflecting their domesticated ancestors.

Feral Cats

Wild Cat

Introduction

HOW TO OBSERVE MAMMALS

One of the most critical factors in mammal watching is the time of day. While some mammals are active day and night, a greater number are active at dawn and dusk than at almost any other time. In fact, dawn is usually best of all, since there are usually few humans abroad at this hour. In order to observe mammals you must be alert for movements at all times, looking far into the distance as well as up close. Mammals such as Ibex, Chamois and deer can best be seen by scanning a mountainside or across a field with a pair of binoculars – 8 x 40 is a good specification for general use – while seals and whales can sometimes be seen with a telescope from a cliff top. Water voles, Stoats and Weasels are among the species that are often seen clearly in the middle distance, oblivious of the human intruder. But shrews, mice and voles can usually be watched scurrying around a hedge bottom only a couple of metres away. As soon as you see a mammal, whether it is a metre or a kilometre away, freeze. Most mammals will ignore, or at least will not run away from, a motionless human figure. Freeze, and then, if the animal you are observing is within earshot, you can try 'squeaking'. This involves making a sucking, or kissing sound, or using a purpose-made mechanical squeaker. Many mammals, particularly carnivores such as weasels, but occasionally other species such as hares and squirrels, are fascinated by this sound and will approach to investigate the observer. It appears that they think the sound is made by an injured animal.

Looking under sheets of corrugated iron, timber and logs (remembering to replace them all carefully) is a good way of seeing most small mammals such as voles and shrews. Their nests and runs can be found in such places, together with caches of food. The nests of Harvest Mice can be most readily found in tall grass around hedges and reed beds in late summer. Wood Mice often build feeding platforms in old birds' nests, and the untidy leaf-nests (dreys) of squirrels are easily spotted in the fork of a tree. Even though their signs are often visible, the majority of mammals are largely nocturnal or crepuscular. Bats are among the most difficult to observe, but a wide range of mammals can be seen at night using a spotlight or powerful torch. Even better is a parallel focus beam lamp that plugs into the dashboard of a car. When driving around country lanes, you may sight mammals such as deer, foxes, hedgehogs, rabbits and hares in the car headlights. The chances of seeing such mammals are dramatically increased by reducing your speed when driving in the countryside. Most mammals will ignore a car, enabling you to stop and watch. A quiet walk in woodland or along a hedgerow using a torch with a red filter, listening for rustling leaves, is another exceptionally good way of seeing mammals. It is important to note the height of the eyes from the ground, and the distance between them in order to gauge the animal's size. Note also the colour of the eyeshine.

Finally, patience is a virtue that is sometimes rewarded with good views of the shyer mammals. Most mammals rely fairly heavily on their sense of smell, so provided you are concealed downwind from a badger sett, or the feeding glade of deer, you stand a good chance of seeing them. Being concealed does not necessarily mean being in a hide – the mere presence of such an intrusive object disturbs wildlife and may take several days to be accepted. Standing against a tree so that your outline is not obvious is often just as effective. Wear subdued clothing in which you can move about quietly, and avoid carrying metallic objects that will glint in the sun.

Recording your observations in a notebook will make identification easier when looking through your field guide later. This should be done without delay as it is easy to forget small details.

Handling mammals

Live trapping is one of the few reliable ways of seeing many small species of mammal. A wide range of safe live traps is now available, and many wildlife societies and field centres organise study groups and training for enthusiasts. Initially, trapping should only be carried out under supervision, since many species are protected by law, and unless great care is taken, mammals can be killed needlessly, even in live traps. The use of nets for trapping bats is strictly controlled in Britain and most other parts of Europe, and can be carried out only under the direct supervision of a licensed bat worker.

All wild mammals should be handled with care, and only after training by an experienced mammalogist. Most species carry a wide range of diseases, a few of which are dangerous to humans. Despite widespread publicity, rabies is unlikely to be encountered through handling mammals, and is not known to occur in Britain, but never take risks. Never handle mammals without gloves, and in particular, do not touch any mammal that appears to be sick or dying.

Introduction

HOW TO IDENTIFY MAMMALS

Once you are familiar with the general characteristics of the main groups, mammals can be identified with relative ease at this level. First impressions are often very important, for instance rabbits and hares, with their long ears, are easily distinguished from even the largest rodents. However, the critical features for distinguishing between closely related species differ for each group. The most obvious characteristics – size and colour – are often the least helpful as there may be considerable variation within a species, and similarity between species. Because of the diversity of mammals a wide range of techniques is often needed to identify them to the species level. Since many are nocturnal or secretive, a certain amount of detective work is also needed. Scents, sounds, food remains, burrows, nests and droppings can all be used to identify mammals.

This section points out which features or measurements are important when making an identification within a particular group. Knowing which particular characteristics to note allows an accurate identification of many species to be made from even a brief sighting, or simply from the signs a mammal leaves behind. If you see an animal disappearing into the bushes, remember to examine the place you saw it last for footprints, hairs and other signs.

Measurements
Often the best way to be sure of a mammal's identity is to take detailed measurements. Although the critical measurements vary from group to group, the following are the most important: head and body length, tail length (measured from the base to the tip, but excluding hairs), ear length, length of hind foot (excluding claws), and weight. The length of the hind foot is particularly useful in the case of shrews and mice as there is little variation between different age groups. The forearm length of bats is often critical, as is the ear length and wingspan. Cetaceans and pinnipeds do not have the tail visibly distinct from the body, so an overall measurement is given. In the case of feral and domestic mammals there is often considerable variation. A summary of the measurements for each species is given in the fact panels.

Detailed measurements are needed to identify most small mammals. When measuring the ears and feet of species such as shrews, a pair of callipers or dividers is needed.

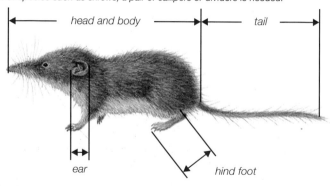

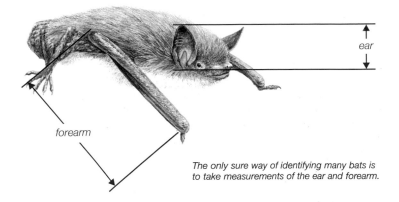

The only sure way of identifying many bats is to take measurements of the ear and forearm.

Dentition

The teeth are often a very important aid to the identification of mammals. The dental formula gives the count of the teeth in one upper and one lower jaw. For example,

$$\frac{1.0.0.3}{1.0.0.3}$$

indicates that there is one incisor, no canines or premolars, and three molars – a typical rodent. A question mark indicates that a tooth may be present or absent, and 2–4 indicates that the number varies between two and four teeth. The dentition of cetaceans is particularly variable, and many species of whales lack teeth completely; they are replaced with plates of horny 'baleen', which are used to filter zooplankton. In some of the toothed whales, only the males have teeth; in others they are present only occasionally and are presumably non-functional.

Sounds

The study of mammal sounds is comparatively recent for most species but it is beginning to be used for identification purposes. Some mammals can be heard in the breeding season – foxes are often particularly vocal. Red Deer 'bell' – a sort of belching call – seals bark, and cats purr.

Bats use echolocation for navigation and make a wide range of mostly ultrasonic calls. In order to listen to frequencies above the range of human hearing, bat-detectors have been developed. These electronic devices convert the sounds into audible signals. When sound ranges are given in this book the starting frequencies are given first – the calls of many bats start high and sweep down, whereas many cetaceans start low and rise. Shrews and many other mammals have a wide range of squeaks and other calls, including ultrasounds, but they have not been studied in detail. As with most descriptions of animal sounds, transcription is difficult, and a degree of imagination is needed in order to interpret a written description.

Some mammals will respond to a tape recording in the same way as territorial birds, moving closer in order to drive off the 'intruder', and thus provide an opportunity to observe them. However, this technique is not advisable in the case of large mammals such as deer, as they can be very aggressive in the rut.

Introduction

Insectivores
Hedgehogs are among Europe's most familiar mammals, but are unfortunately encountered more often as road casualties than alive. They are covered with spines and look rather ungainly, though they are surprisingly agile. Unlike most other insectivores, hedgehogs hibernate.

The shrews found in Europe are all fairly small, and include one of the world's smallest mammals, the Pygmy White-toothed Shrew, which might be mistaken for a furry beetle!

The individual species of moles and hedgehogs are best distinguished by their ranges, except in the relatively small areas of overlap, where measurements are used. The shrews are more difficult to identify – in some cases this is virtually impossible in the field. Again, range is extremely important. The water shrews are relatively easy to distinguish, but in mainland Europe the Common Shrew and its close relatives are often extremely confusing. Dead specimens and skulls found in the pellets of birds of prey are often easier to identify, as differences in tooth structure can be distinguished using a hand lens.

Bats
Bats are among the most difficult of all Europe's mammals to identify. Even in the hand several species can only normally be identified by detailed measurements and close examination. The shape and size of the ears and tragus (ear-lobe) is often important and in some species the colour of the fur may also help. The horseshoe-bats have elaborate appendages on their noses, and each species has a characteristic profile. The calcar is a bone extending out from the ankle of many bats to support the wing membrane, and in pipistrelles the presence of a post calcarial lobe – a small web of skin – is an aid to identification.

In flight most bats are almost impossible to identify with any certainty, but with the interest in bats rapidly increasing, and a large number of amateur and professional enthusiasts observing them, field identification techniques have been steadily improving. Many species have distinctive sound patterns and tape cassette guides enable several species to be identified accurately using a bat detector.

It should be noted that in Britain and many other countries in Europe, bats are strictly protected by law and a licence is required to handle them.

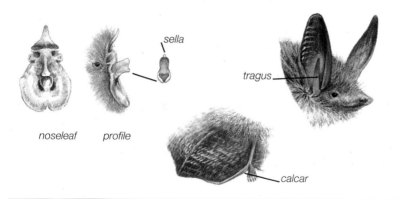

noseleaf   profile   sella   tragus   calcar

Introduction

Rodents and lagomorphs
Although most rodents are relatively distinctive, and can be identified conclusively by their skulls, some can be separated only by differences in their chromosomes or DNA. The pine voles are among the most difficult, and European species of house mice have only recently been separated. The lagomorphs can be distinguished by their size, the colour and length of the ears and the colour of the tail, but range is also important. They leave distinctive footprints and their droppings are usually characteristic pellets of grass.

Many rodents and lagomorphs are extremely prolific, often reproducing within a few weeks of birth. House mice and Brown Rats, for example, can soon build up to plague proportions. Voles and lemmings are often cyclical, particularly in the north, building up huge populations, which then crash. When they are at their peak the population can be so dense that it appears to almost carpet the ground, and can strip it bare of vegetation. When rodents or lagomorphs are abundant, the numbers of predatory mammals (and birds) often increase dramatically.

Mountain Hare   *Brown Hare*

Carnivores
Most carnivores are relatively large and are often easily identified. They can also be detected by the signs they leave, such as droppings and footprints, which are also characteristic. The majority of carnivores have thick fur; the dense, soft underfur is often protected by longer, coarser guard hairs. In some species, such as the Otter, the guard hairs form a waterproof coat.

The predatory habits of carnivores have led to their widespread persecution. Consequently they tend to be rather shy. They are less numerous than small mammals such as insectivores and rodents, and are therefore relatively rarely seen in most parts of Europe. However, there are exceptions. The Red Fox, for example has adapted to suburban areas, and is often seen in car headlights as it trots from one rubbish bin to another in search of food. In other areas Pine Martens are spreading, and where they are not persecuted Badgers become remarkably tame and make regular visits to suburban gardens to be fed.

Primates
Only one species of primate other than humans is found in Europe – the Barbary Ape or Macaque. It is almost certainly not native to Europe, but is well established on Gibraltar, where its only European population has been recorded for several centuries. It is not a true ape, but is so called because it lacks a tail. It is gregarious, living in troops, and is unlikely to be confused with any other species.

Introduction

Pinnipeds
Of the three families of pinnipeds – sea lions, seals and the Walrus – only the last two occur in European waters, although there have been reports of sea lion escapes (or abandoned circus animals) surviving in the Mediterranean. Although they are mostly marine, Common and Ringed Seals are also found in estuaries and rivers, often far inland, and the Ringed Seal occurs in a few land-locked lakes. The Walrus is only very rarely seen outside the extreme north.

In water usually only the head can be seen, and identification is difficult. However, some species have distinctive profiles, such as the 'Roman nose' of the Grey Seal. Seals are most easily identified on land, when they have 'hauled out' on beaches, although there is considerable variation in colour and markings within species. The Walrus is easily distinguished by its large size, bristled upper lip, and tusks, which are found on all males and also some females.

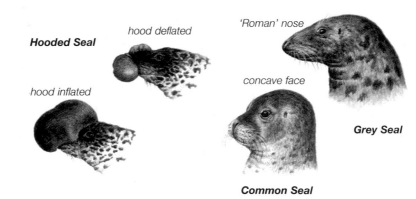

Ungulates
Deer and other ungulates are the largest of the grazing and browsing animals in Europe. They are mostly found in woodland, emerging to graze in pastures and meadows at night, but also occur in a few more open habitats such as moorlands. The males of all European deer (except the introduced Chinese Water Deer) carry antlers, as does the female Reindeer. The size and shape of the antlers of adult deer is very distinctive. Some deer have relatively simple, spiky antlers, while others are large and branching. The antlers start to grow in summer, and are covered in a velvet skin which is rich in blood vessels. In autumn, when they are full size, the velvet dries and is then rubbed off, exposing the hard, bony antlers in time for the breeding season or rut. The following spring the antlers are shed. The other bovids such as Ibex, the Chamois and the Mouflon, do not shed their horns; these continue to grow for most of the animal's life.

The rut of deer is usually in late summer or autumn. The males of some species gather harems and defend territories, but others are less sociable. The distinctive grunts, whistles and bellows of the males can often be heard during the rut. Ibex can be heard clashing horns for a considerable distance across mountain valleys.

Although the footprints of deer are often obvious on wet ground, they can be difficult to identify due to the overlap in size between the various age groups of different species. However, it is usually possible to identify deer and other bovids from their tracks when they are found in combination with other features. The most obvious are droppings, browse lines, where bark has been stripped from the trees, and wallows.

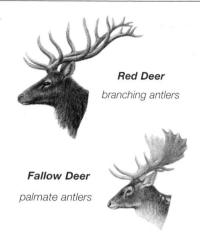

Red Deer
branching antlers

Fallow Deer
palmate antlers

Cetaceans

Cetaceans are rarely observed, since they are almost entirely marine, and seldom come close to shore. Most species are also rare, due to over-hunting and a range of environmental problems such as tangling in fishing gear, swallowing polythene bags and chemical pollution.

Cetaceans are occasionally found on beaches, stranded when the tide goes out and they cannot swim back out to sea. The reason why they come near to the shore and stay there when it is clearly dangerous to do so, has not been adequately resolved. Because of their often well-developed social behaviour, whole family groups or even schools become stranded as they try to help each other. Stranded whales are generally easy to identify, as they can be measured and the teeth or baleen can be examined. Stranded whales should also be reported to the local coastguard.

Although the whole whale is rarely seen above the surface, it is possible

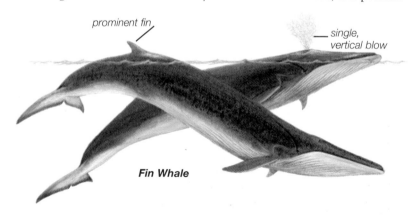

prominent fin

single, vertical blow

Fin Whale

to identify the species from a brief glimpse of the back or tail. Important features to look for are the position of the dorsal fin and its shape and size. The blow is often distinctive, with the height, shape, direction, clarity and duration varying between each species. Some whales expose the tail flukes, and the way they dive or breach (break the surface) is often characteristic. The best way of seeing cetaceans is on boat trips organized for whale watching.

Introduction

TRACKS AND SIGNS

Recognizing mammals from their tracks and signs is a useful skill to develop. Because mammals are so difficult to observe, knowledge about their distribution is often gained through finding such signs. A number of useful signs to look out for are given below.

Skulls and teeth
Most European mammals can be identified from their skulls, and in many cases from a single jawbone. Skulls and teeth of small mammals can be found in the pellets of birds of prey. Many small mammals also enter discarded bottles and drink cans, becoming trapped, and then die and decompose, leaving behind their bones. The skulls and teeth of many of the smaller species are illustrated, to aid in their identification. However, more detailed keys can be obtained from some of the organizations listed on page 192.

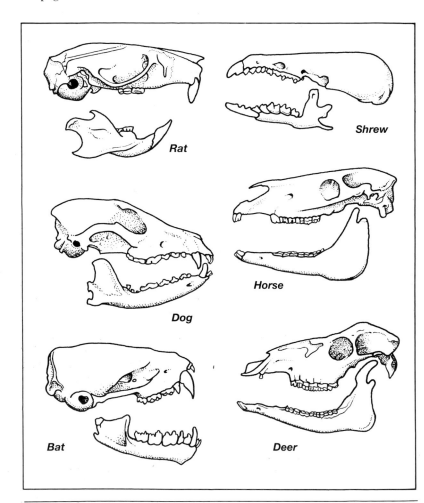

Introduction

Scents

Mammals have distinctive scents, which they frequently use to recognize each other. It is occasionally possible to identify mammals by their smell. This is particularly true of foxes – they leave a distinctive musky odour that can sometimes be detected after they have crossed a path. The scent of Otters' droppings can be used to distinguish them from mink. But scents are difficult to describe, and identifying mammals by smell is a skill which takes time to acquire.

Footprints

The footprints of many species are reasonably distinctive, and with practice they can be identified in the field. Deer and other hoofed animals often leave clear tracks in soft ground or snow. Allowance should be made for the speed at which an animal was travelling – this determines the distance between the prints. If it had jumped, the hooves or pads may be splayed. Knowledge of behaviour can be important in identifying tracks – a dog will wander around, whereas the fox, which has similar prints, leaves a direct trail. Even small mammals such as mice and shrews leave impressions and their tracks are usually visible in snow and mud in woodland.

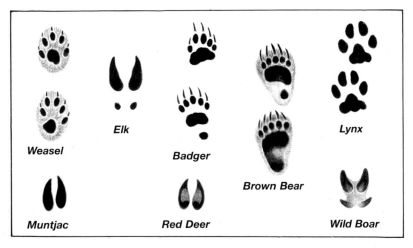

Weasel   **Elk**   **Badger**   **Brown Bear**   **Lynx**

Muntjac   **Red Deer**   **Wild Boar**

Food remains

Mammals can often be identified by the remains left after a meal. An untidy pile of bird and mammal remains outside a burrow indicates a fox earth, and a Songthrush nest full of the chewed remains of hawthorn berries has probably been used by a Wood Mouse. Squirrels attack pine cones in a distinctive manner, and hazel nuts eaten by dormice show characteristic chisel-like gnaw marks.

hazel nut gnawed by Hazel Doormouse

hazel nut gnawed by squirrel

Introduction

Droppings
Most larger mammals can be identified fairly accurately by their droppings (also known as scats). Since these are often associated with both food remains and footprints it is likely that the combination of signs will give an accurate identification.

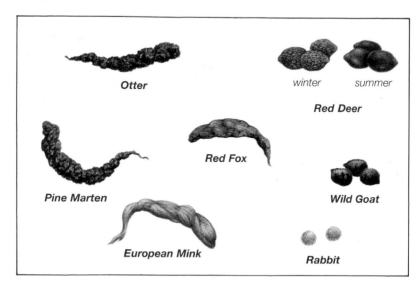

Otter

winter   *summer*

Red Deer

Red Fox

Pine Marten

Wild Goat

European Mink

Rabbit

The droppings of mice and other rodents are small oval pellets that comprise the fibrous remains of plant material. Bat and insectivore droppings are similar in size and shape, but since they include the remains of their prey, shiny beetle elytra (wing cases), insect legs and the remains of worms are usually visible. The droppings of rabbits, hares and deer are larger pellets. Those of deer may vary according to diet; in summer when they feed on grass, they produce larger, softer droppings that resemble small cow pats. The elongate droppings of carnivores usually include fur and occasionally bone, and are often deposited on rocks, ant hills and other prominent places.

Bats can be particularly difficult to detect, but their droppings are often clearly visible on the altar cloths and pews in a church, indicating their presence. Urine staining around a hole or crevice often indicates the roost, and an accumulation of droppings and insect wings in a porch indicates a feeding station.

Territorial markings
Many mammals are highly territorial, and while most use scent to mark their territory, some use more obvious markers. For example, deer have 'fraying stocks'. They damage shrubs and trees by rubbing them with their antlers. Some mammals, in particular carnivores, leave their droppings in prominent positions, and these are sometimes distinctively scented. Otters, for example, leave their rather sweet smelling 'spraints' on rocks and promontories.

Nests and burrows

The burrows of many mammals are easy to spot, particularly if there are footprints and other signs close by. They range in size from the Beaver's lodge to the tiny ball-sized nest of the Harvest Mouse. The large setts used by Badgers usually have well-trodden paths radiating from them, with dung pits several metres away. Moles, ground squirrels and water voles all have recognizable burrows.

Many small mammals make their nests under fallen logs, stones or rubbish. Sheets of corrugated iron are particularly good places to search – these sites are often shared with snakes and other wildlife. Several species of mammals may share the same runs and burrows. The tiny runs in a hedgerow may be used by voles and shrews, and by the Weasels that prey on them.

Beaver lodge

nest of Hazel Dormouse

Other signs

Rubbing and scratching posts are a useful guide to the identification of many mammals. Note the height at which the bark is removed, plus any hairs which may be caught. Badgers leave deep scratches in the bark of trees as they clean their long claws. Larger mammals rub against the trunk, removing patches of bark. Short, thick, dark hairs are left by deer on trees and fences, and rabbit hair is often found on bushes. Black and silver hairs caught on barbed wire show where a Badger has brushed against it. Other common signs are scratch marks made by carnivores keeping their claws in trim, and the gnawing of rodents and lagomorphs. The massive, chisel-like tooth marks of a Beaver are distinctive, and the neatly chopped twigs about 50cm (20in) or more off the ground are the result of hares browsing. The flattened sleeping places of deer and other large mammals are often seen clearly in the undergrowth, and even the 'form' where a hare rests can sometimes be detected. In winter many mammals live beneath the snow, often for several months, and their runs, nests and food remains are clearly visible when it thaws.

Badger hairs

tree stump gnawed by Beaver

Introduction

BEHAVIOUR AND LIFE CYCLE

A brief outline of the main behavioural characteristics is given in the fact panel, and a glance at this section will give an indication of the time of day a species is most likely to be encountered. Certain behavioural traits may also be useful for identification, such as breathing patterns in the case of cetaceans. Many mammals hibernate in order to save energy when food is in short supply over winter, and the period of hibernation is given, together with the external temperature in the case of bats. Most mammals are relatively sedentary, but migration patterns are given where applicable. Cetaceans undergo seasonal migrations, and consequently are more likely to be seen in spring and autumn.

The details given in the fact panels under the section on life cycle are subject to much regional variation, particularly in the case of those mammals with an extensive range. Animals living in the north and at high altitudes generally breed later than those in the south. Hence the references to spring, summer and autumn refer to the local conditions and not to any particular months. Surprisingly, data on the life cycle of many species is scant, particularly relating to the age of sexual maturity. This may vary widely, with males maturing at a different time to females. In cases where there is no information available on litter size, the young or maturity, the figures will generally be similar to closely related species, although there are exceptions. There is considerable variation in the size and number of vole litters, and it is likely that the age of maturity and longevity also vary as a consequence.

The Humpback Whale can be recognized by its distinctive behaviour. It frequently breaches, playfully slapping the water with its fins and performing back somersaults.

Longevity

Many mammals live far longer in captivity than they would in the wild. For the majority of mammals the maximum life expectancy, even in the wild, is considerably greater than the average life expectancy. The average is usually quite low due to high juvenile mortality. For many species there is little or no data for life expectancy in the wild. Where such data is available, this book gives the maximum life expectancy for each species.

Introduction

MAMMALS AND PEOPLE

The human race has had greater effect on the mammals than on any other group of animals in Europe. Throughout human history mammals have been hunted, for food, for their fur, or for sport. This has resulted in the widespread decline of many species and the extinction of others, such as the Bison, Brown Bear and many deer, over much of their former range.

Carnivores have been subject to widespread persecution in Europe. Wolves are on the brink of extinction, largely because of campaigns waged against them on account of their depredations of livestock. Lynx and martens have been hunted both because they occasionally prey on poultry and other livestock, and also because their fur was highly valued. Even small carnivores such as polecats, Weasels and Stoats have been trapped extensively by gamekeepers seeking to increase stocks of pheasants and other game birds.

The ungulates have been affected more than any other group of mammals. Several species have been exterminated and then reintroduced, others have been enclosed and farmed. Deer are selectively culled and are artificially fed in winter, in order to preserve stocks for the hunting season. Several exotic, mainly oriental, species have been introduced.

Few marine mammals have escaped persecution. Extensive whaling has reduced numbers of Blue, Sei, Fin, Humpback and Bowhead Whales to the point of extinction. Until quite recently, seals were widespread and often abundant in most of the seas around Europe. The Mediterranean Monk Seal was once widespread from the Atlantic to the Black Sea. It is now one of the world's rarest mammals, and is unlikely to survive long into the 21st century. The Grey Seal survives in substantial numbers only in Scottish and Irish waters, and populations in the Atlantic, North Sea and Baltic Seas are seriously threatened.

Technological developments have caused further decline in mammal numbers, through destruction of their habitats. As forests are cleared, many of the inhabitants are lost, unless, like the Red Fox and Raccoon, they can adapt to urban habitats. Polluted waterways are another problem, and numbers of Otters have recently dropped in many parts of Europe as a result.

Because of the drastic decline of so many species, and the disappearance of others, many mammals are protected in most parts of Europe, and several organizations are also campaigning to protect the habitats on which their survival depends. The main legislation covering wild mammals in the United Kingdom is the Wildlife and Countryside Act (1981 and subsequent amendments). Under this Act the Badger, Otter, Red Squirrel, Hedgehog, Wild Cat, Polecat and Pine Marten, all bats, dolphins and porpoises, shrews and dormice receive varying degrees of protection. In particular, it is illegal to capture or kill any of them. In fact, bats in the roof space of a house may not be disturbed. Deer, seals and whales are also protected under special laws. However, in spite of the measures so far taken, many mammals are still seriously threatened and international legislation is required in order to ensure their survival.

Glossary

Baleen plates (of whales) horny plates with fibrous edges on the upper jaw, used to filter plankton and small fish.

Beech mast nuts of beech trees.

Breach (of whales) break through the surface of the water.

Callosity an abnormally thick piece of skin.

Calcar (of bats) small bone extending along the edge of the tail membrane.

Caravanning (of shrews) behaviour where the young follow each other behind the mother.

Crepuscular active at dawn and/or dusk.

Discontinuous range patchy distribution, with populations separated usually by tracts of unsuitable habitat.

Diurnal active during the day.

Drey squirrel's nest.

Echolocation mechanism used by bats and cetaceans to navigate by means of sound pulses and their echoes – also known as sonar.

Feral domesticated animals that have reverted to the wild.

Gleaning (of bats) picking insects off leaves while hovering.

Haul out place where seals come ashore.

Krill general word for zooplankton, particularly crustaceans.

Localized distribution small, scattered populations.

Myriapods centipedes and millipedes.

Nocturnal active at night.

Noseleaf (of bats) elaborate skin structure on the nose, used in echolocation.

Palmate (of antlers) hand-like.

Pelage fur (coat).

Pod group of whales.

Post-canine teeth behind the canines.

Prehensile (of tails) adapted for grasping.

Rorqual fast-swimming whale of the genus Balaenoptera.

Rufous reddish.

Rut breeding season.

Scut short, white tail of rabbits, deer etc., flashed as warning.

Sella central lobe on the noseleaf of bats.

Taiga coniferous forest belt stretching from the edge of the Arctic to the deciduous woodlands and steppes to the south.

Tragus (of bats) ear lobe growing upwards from the lower edge of the ear, useful in identification.

Translocation moving animals from one area to another, usually for the purpose of introduction or reintrodution.

Tump mound of earth from tunnelling, particularly by moles.

Tundra treeless vegetation zone of the Artic consisting of mosses, lichens and dwarf shrubs.

Unicuspid tooth with only a single crown or cusp.

Vestigial so small as to be almost non-existent.

Zooplankton floating animal life.

MAMMALS

OF BRITAIN & EUROPE

Hedgehog *Erinaceus europaeus*

pale underside

E. concolor

E. europaeus

parting in spines

E. algirus

HEDGEHOG

Type hedgehog
Habitat open woodland, gardens, hedgerows
Status widespread, often abundant

PHYSICAL DETAILS

Head & Body 8.7–31cm
Tail 2–4cm
Weight up to 1.4kg
Teeth $\frac{3.1.3.3}{2.1.2.3}$
Colour brown with paler spines and dark face

FOOD AND HABITS

Food mostly invertebrates, also eggs, young mammals, carrion
Nest dry leaves and grasses in dense cover
Behaviour mostly nocturnal; very agile, also climbs and swims
Voice wide range of grunts and snorts
Hibernation autumn–early spring; in nest
Migration none

LIFE CYCLE

Litters 1 or 2 a year; summer–early autumn
Young 4–5; helpless, with soft spines
Maturity year following birth
Longevity up to 10 years

A familiar, spiny animal that rolls into a ball when attacked, presenting the attacker with a mass of prickles.
Range: most of Europe except extreme north; it has adapted particularly well to suburban habitats. The occurrence of hedgehogs in Finland, as well as Ireland and other islands is almost certainly as a result of introduction by man.
Similar Species: the Eastern Hedgehog (*E. concolor*) which has a pale throat occurs from Eastern Europe to Central Asia. The Algerian Hedgehog (*E. algirus = Atelerix algirus*) is identified by a distinctive 'parting' on its head. Originating in North Africa it is now established in the Balearic Isles and Malta. It has been introduced into mainland Europe, but may be extinct in France.

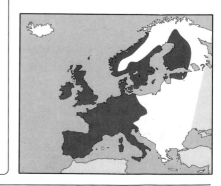

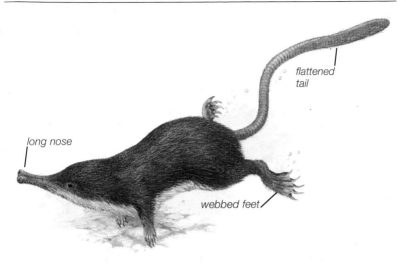

long nose

flattened tail

webbed feet

An aquatic mole with several remarkable adaptations to living in fast-flowing mountain streams. The long snout (2cm) can be used like a snorkel, the powerful hind feet are webbed, and the tail is slightly flattened to act as a rudder. It is mostly nocturnal, spending the day in vole runs and crevices, and sleeping in grass nests. It consumes at least two-thirds of its body weight a day, feeding on aquatic insects and their larvae, other invertebrates and small fish.

Range: confined to the Pyrenees of France and Spain, and the Cantabrians of Spain and Portugal.

Similar Species: water shrews, which are smaller and black; water voles, which are rarely found in fast-flowing streams; rats, which swim with most of their body on the surface of the water.

PYRENEAN DESMAN

Type	mole
Habitat	fast-flowing streams
Status	threatened throughout range

PHYSICAL DETAILS

Head & Body	11–16.6cm
Tail	12.6–15.6cm
Weight	50–80g
Teeth	3.1.4.3 3.1.4.3
Colour	dark brown above with glossy sheen, paler below

FOOD AND HABITS

Food	aquatic invertebrates, small fish
Nest	in holes or among crevices
Behaviour	mostly nocturnal; swims and dives
Voice	unknown
Hibernation	none
Migration	none

LIFE CYCLE

Litters	usually 1 a year; summer
Young	1–5, usually 4; naked and helpless
Maturity	second year
Longevity	over 3 years

Blind Mole *Talpa caeca*

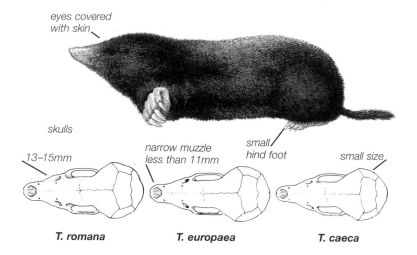

eyes covered with skin

skulls

13–15mm

narrow muzzle less than 11mm

small hind foot

small size

T. romana   **T. europaea**   **T. caeca**

BLIND MOLE

Type	mole
Habitat	grassland, woodland, up to 2000m
Status	little known, but not threatened

PHYSICAL DETAILS

Head & Body	9–14cm
Tail	2.7–3cm
Hindfoot	less than 1.7cm
Weight	30–70g
Teeth	$\frac{3.1.4.3}{3.1.4.3}$
Colour	grey-black, with pinkish paws and muzzle

FOOD AND HABITS

Food	invertebrates, particularly earthworms
Nest	presumed similar to Common Mole
Behaviour	alternately active and resting throughout 24 hours
Voice	unknown
Hibernation	none
Migration	none

LIFE CYCLE

Litters	1 in spring
Young	2–6; naked and helpless
Maturity	no data
Longevity	no data

The smallest European mole, with eyes permanently covered by a membrane. Its hind foot is usually less than 1.7cm long. Otherwise it is superficially identical to other moles.
Range: confined to the Mediterranean region in Iberia, the maritime Alps of France, south of the Alps in Italy; and the Balkans; may also occur in Turkey. The Spanish population of the Blind Mole is now considered a separate species (*T. occidentalis*), as is the population in Croatia, Albania and north-western Greece (*T. stankovici*). They are virtually indistinguishable from other Blind Moles in the field.
Similar Species: the Roman Mole (*T. romana*) also has permanently closed eyes, but it is larger, has a wider muzzle (see skulls), and its hind feet are over 1.75cm long. It is confined to Italy.

molehills

Moles are unlikely to be confused with any other mammals, but the three species in Europe are very difficult to separate. A mole spends most of its life underground, and its presence is often known only by mole hills or 'tumps'. It digs extensive networks of tunnels to hunt for earthworms, insects and their larvae, molluscs and myriapods. Surplus prey is stored, having been immobilized by mutilation. Moles have many adaptations to their subterranean life: massive shovel-like forepaws, velvety fur, which brushes in any direction, and reduced eyes.

Range: widespread over most of Europe except for the extreme north and south, and Ireland.

Similar Species: the Roman Mole (*T. romana*) and the Blind Mole (*T. caeca*) are similar but in both species the eyes are permanently closed.

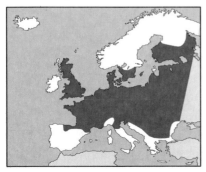

COMMON MOLE
Type	mole
Habitat	mostly grassland; also deciduous woodland; often considered a pest
Status	common

PHYSICAL DETAILS
Head & Body	11.3–15.9cm
Tail	2.5–4cm
Hindfoot	1.7–1.95cm
Weight	72–128g
Teeth	$\frac{3.1.4.3}{3.1.4.3}$
Colour	grey-black with pink paws and muzzle

FOOD AND HABITS
Food	invertebrates, particularly earthworms
Nest	grasses, often inside larger mound or 'fortress'
Behaviour	alternately active and resting throughout 24 hours
Voice	squeaks when fighting
Hibernation	none
Migration	may move out of low-lying meadows in winter to avoid flooding

LIFE CYCLE
Litters	usually 1 a year; summer
Young	3–4; naked and helpless
Maturity	year following birth
Longevity	c3 years

Common Shrew *Sorex araneus*

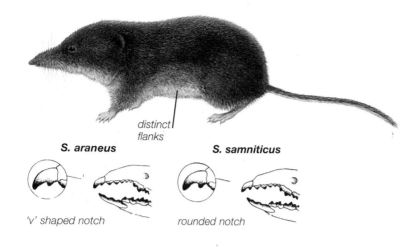

distinct flanks

S. araneus

'v' shaped notch

S. samniticus

rounded notch

	COMMON SHREW
Type	shrew
Habitat	almost all areas with ground cover
Status	not threatened; often abundant

PHYSICAL DETAILS

Head & Body	5.5–8.5cm
Tail	3.4–4.7cm
Weight	4.8–14g
Teeth	3.1.3.3
	2.0.1.3
Colour	chocolate-brown above, paler below

FOOD AND HABITS

Food	invertebrates
Nest	grasses, underground
Behaviour	alternately resting and active throughout 24 hours; usually scurries in runs
Voice	squeaks; often heard in hedges
Hibernation	none
Migration	none

LIFE CYCLE

Litters	up to 5 a year; spring–autumn
Young	5–7; naked and helpless
Maturity	normally year following birth
Longevity	less than 2 years

An abundant and widespread small insectivore. Its fur is tri-coloured, being dark brown above and pale below, and separated by a distinctive intermediate band. The teeth are red-tipped.
Range: common over much of northern and eastern Europe.
Similar Species: Millet's Shrew (*S. coronatus*) and the Spanish Shrew (*S. granarius*) are almost identical to the Common Shrew and often cannot be distinguished from it except by examining their chromosomes. Millet's Shrew occurs sporadically in western Europe and is also found on Jersey; the Spanish Shrew is confined to the mountains of central Spain. The Appennine Shrew (*S. samniticus*) is also very similar to the Common Shrew, but has a distinctly shorter tail (under 4cm), and a rounded notch in its first tooth. It is confined to southern Italy.

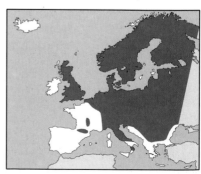

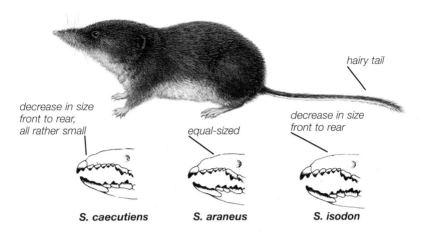

decrease in size front to rear, all rather small

hairy tail

equal-sized

decrease in size front to rear

S. caecutiens   **S. araneus**   **S. isodon**

Laxmann's or the Masked Shrew is a red-toothed shrew, intermediate in size between the Common Shrew (*S. araneus*) and the Pygmy Shrew (*S. minutus*), but with a more contrastingly pale belly, and ears longer than 7mm (the Pygmy Shrew's ears are less than 6.5mm).
Range: confined to northern Scandinavia and Finland, with relict populations in Poland and other parts of eastern Europe. Outside Europe it extends across Asia to Japan.
Similar Species: the Dusky Shrew (*S. isodon=sinalis*) occurs mostly within the same range as Laxmann's, but is a relatively large species that is very similar to the Common Shrew. It differs from the latter by having a considerably darker belly. The Dusky Shrew was first discovered in Finland in 1949 and in Norway in 1968.

LAXMANN'S SHREW

Type	shrew
Habitat	woodland, tundra, taiga
Status	little known

PHYSICAL DETAILS

Head & Body	4.8–7cm
Tail	3–4.6cm
Weight	3–8.5g
Teeth	$\frac{3.1.3.3}{2.0.1.3}$
Colour	brown above, greyish below

FOOD AND HABITS

Food	mostly invertebrates
Nest	grasses in burrow
Behaviour	alternately active and resting throughout 24 hours
Voice	high-pitched squeaks
Hibernation	none
Migration	none

LIFE CYCLE

Litters	1 or 2 a year; spring–summer
Young	2–11; naked and helpless
Maturity	year following birth
Longevity	probably less than 2 years

Pygmy Shrew *Sorex minutus*

long tail

PYGMY SHREW

Type	shrew
Habitat	almost all areas with ground cover
Status	not threatened

PHYSICAL DETAILS

Head & Body	3.9–6.4cm
Tail	3.2–4.4cm
Weight	2–6.3g
Teeth	3.1.3.3
	2.0.1.3
Colour	brown above, paler below

FOOD AND HABITS

Food	invertebrates
Nest	woven from dry grasses
Behaviour	alternately active and resting throughout 24 hours; usually in runs or underground
Voice	squeaks
Hibernation	none
Migration	none

LIFE CYCLE

Litters	at least 2 a year, often 3 or 4; spring–autumn
Young	2–12; naked and helpless
Maturity	year following birth; some the same year
Longevity	less than 2 years

A very small shrew with a proportionally long, thick tail. It is brown above, pale below, and lighter in colour than the Common Shrew (*S. araneus*). Like all Sorex shrews, the teeth are red-tipped, and its skull can best be distinguished from that of the Common Shrew and its close relatives by the size of its fourth tooth (third unicuspid). Pygmy Shrews are found in an even wider range of habitats than the Common Shrew, but they are usually less densely populated.
Range: the most widespread species of shrew in Europe, found over most of the continent but absent from much of Iberia and most Mediterranean islands.
Similar Species: the Pygmy White-toothed Shrew (*Suncus etruscus*) lacks pigment in the teeth, and the Least Shrew (*Sorex minutissimus*) has much smaller hind feet.

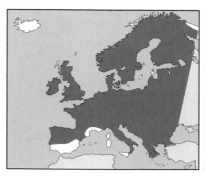

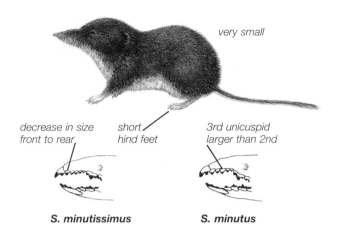

very small

decrease in size front to rear   *short hind feet*   *3rd unicuspid larger than 2nd*

S. minutissimus   **S. minutus**

A tiny shrew with red-tipped teeth, found mostly in coniferous woodland. It is most readily identified by its very small size, and its particularly short hind feet (less than 9mm). Its tail is proportionally shorter than that of the Pygmy Shrew (*S. minutus*).
Range: Russia eastward through Siberia to Japan. In Europe it is confined to parts of Scandinavia, Estonia and the USSR; it may be more widespread, particularly in Scandinavia. Its recognition as a separate species in Europe is comparatively recent (1960).
Similar Species: the Pygmy Shrew, which is bigger, with a third unicuspid tooth that is larger than the second; the Pygmy White-toothed Shrew (*Suncus etruscus*), which does not have red-tipped teeth.

LEAST SHREW

Type	shrew
Habitat	coniferous forest
Status	little known

PHYSICAL DETAILS

Head & Body	3.5–4.5cm
Tail	2.1–3.2cm
Weight	1.5–4g
Teeth	$\frac{3.1.3.3}{2.0.1.3}$
Colour	greyish brown

FOOD AND HABITS

Food	invertebrates
Nest	probably grasses
Behaviour	alternately active and resting throughout 24 hours
Voice	high-pitched squeaks
Hibernation	none
Migration	presumed none

LIFE CYCLE

Litters	1 or 2 a year; summer
Young	3–6; naked and helpless
Maturity	45 days
Longevity	no data

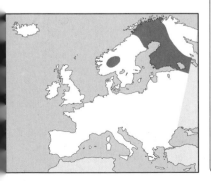

Alpine Shrew *Sorex alpinus*

jawbones

long tail

dark
underside

ALPINE SHREW	
Type	shrew
Habitat	mostly coniferous forest, often near water
Status	not threatened

PHYSICAL DETAILS

Head & Body	5.9–8.3cm
Tail	5.6–7.4cm
Weight	5.5–12g
Teeth	$\frac{3.1.3.3}{2.0.1.3}$
Colour	blackish

FOOD AND HABITS

Food	invertebrates
Nest	grasses in burrow
Behaviour	alternately resting and active
Voice	high-pitched squeaks
Hibernation	none
Migration	none

LIFE CYCLE

Litters	1–2 a year; summer
Young	c6; naked and helpless
Maturity	probably year following birth
Longevity	probably less than 2 years

A distinctive dark grey shrew, often almost black, with red-tipped teeth and a long tail. It is relatively large, being intermediate in size between the Common Shrew (*S. araneus*) and Water Shrew (*Neomys fodiens*), and its tail is approximately equal to its head and body length. It mostly occurs in mountain regions at altitudes over 500m, up to the tree-line.

Range: includes the Alps, the Balkans, the Harz and Carpathian Mountains. Although once recorded as occurring in a small area in the Pyrenees, no recent evidence supports this claim.

Similar Species: water shrews, which are often white on the belly and have fringes of hair on the feet and tail. The other shrews are mostly brownish and the Dusky Shrew (*S. isodon=sinalis*), the darkest and most similar in colouring, occurs further north.

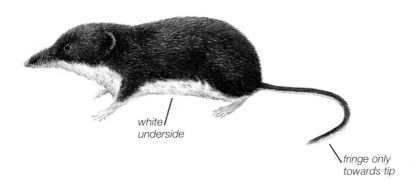

white
underside

fringe only
towards tip

Miller's or the Mediterranean Water Shrew is similar in appearance to the Water Shrew (*N. fodiens*), but is generally slightly smaller, and its belly is almost always white. It also has a fringe of hairs on the last third of its tail, and less well-fringed feet. The ranges of the two shrews often overlap, and they may even share the same river. Miller's Water Shrew is, however, not as aquatic as the Water Shrew.
Range: despite its alternative common name this shrew is not confined to the Mediterranean, but is quite widespread. However, its range is discontinuous, and tends to be associated with mountains, except in eastern Europe where it often occurs in lowlands.
Similar Species: the Water Shrew – see above; the Alpine Shrew (*Sorex alpinus*), which always has a dark belly.

MILLER'S WATER SHREW

Type	shrew
Habitat	wetlands, but less tied to water than Water Shrew
Status	not threatened

PHYSICAL DETAILS

Head & Body	6.7–8.7cm
Tail	4–5.2cm
Weight	8–17g
Teeth	3.1.2.3 1.1.1.3
Colour	black above, white below

FOOD AND HABITS

Food	invertebrates
Nest	in burrow
Behaviour	mostly diurnal
Voice	squeaks
Hibernation	none
Migration	none

LIFE CYCLE

Litters	2 a year; summer
Young	5–12; naked and helpless
Maturity	2–3 months
Longevity	probably less than 2 years

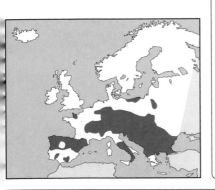

Water Shrew *Neomys fodiens*

fringed tail

underside can be dark

fringed feet

appears silvery under water

WATER SHREW

Type	shrew
Habitat	mostly wetlands
Status	not threatened

PHYSICAL DETAILS

Head & Body	7–9.6cm
Tail	5.1–7.2cm
Weight	11.4–17.5g
Teeth	3.1.2.3 1.1.1.3
Colour	black above; white, grey or black below

FOOD AND HABITS

Food	mostly aquatic invertebrates; also small fish and frogs; its saliva is venomous to small animals
Nest	grasses in burrow
Behaviour	alternately active and resting throughout 24 hours
Voice	squeaks
Hibernation	none
Migration	none

LIFE CYCLE

Litters	2–3 a year; spring–summer
Young	3–9; naked and helpless
Maturity	2–3 months
Longevity	less than 2 years

This is the largest of the European shrews. It is generally black above and white below, although the underside can sometimes be buffy or blackish. The Water Shrew is well adapted to swimming, with a keel of stiff hairs along the tail and on the sides of the hind feet. It dives for up to 20 seconds. Although normally found close to streams, ponds, ditches and other wetland habitats, it is occasionally found far from water.

Range: widespread over most of Europe, but absent from most of Iberia, much of the Balkans, Ireland and most Mediterranean islands.

Similar Species: Miller's Water Shrew (*N. anomalus*), which is slightly smaller with a white belly; the Alpine Shrew (*Sorex alpinus*), which is always uniformly dark, and lacks the fringes of hair on the feet and tail.

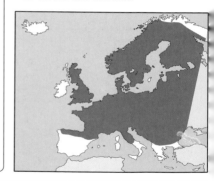

longish hair

pale underside

very small

The Pygmy White-toothed Shrew (also known as Savi's or the Etruscan Shrew) is one of the smallest mammals in the world, and has been likened to a furry beetle! Like other white-toothed shrews, the tail has 'whiskers'. It is often found around human habitations, in open dry woodland, and in scrub and olive groves. It is rarely seen, and much of its distribution is known only from remains in owl pellets.

Range: a wide distribution, which includes Africa and southern Asia. In Europe it is confined to the Mediterranean region, including Sardinia, Corsica, the Balearic Isles, Sicily and many other islands.

Similar Species: the Least Shrew (*Sorex minutissimus*) has red-tipped teeth and occurs only in north-eastern Europe; the Pygmy Shrew (*Sorex minutus*), which is larger.

PYGMY WHITE-TOOTHED SHREW

Type	shrew
Habitat	variable, often around cultivated areas
Status	not threatened

PHYSICAL DETAILS

Head & Body	3.6–5.3cm
Tail	2.1–3cm
Weight	1.2–2.7g
Teeth	3.1.2.3 2.0.1.3
Colour	light brownish

FOOD AND HABITS

Food	spiders, small insects
Nest	grasses, scrub under logs and stones
Behaviour	alternately active and resting throughout 24 hours
Voice	squeaks
Hibernation	can become torpid, but does not hibernate
Migration	none

LIFE CYCLE

Litters	5–6 a year; spring–early autumn
Young	2–6; naked and helpless
Maturity	c2–3 months
Longevity	probably less than 1 year

Greater White-toothed Shrew *Crocidura russula*

prominent
whiskers
on tail

GREATER WHITE-TOOTHED SHREW

Type	shrew
Habitat	variable; includes scrub, gardens, vineyards
Status	not threatened

PHYSICAL DETAILS

Head & Body	6–9cm
Tail	3–4.6cm
Weight	5.9–11.3g
Teeth	3.1.1.3
	2.0.1.3
Colour	grey-brown

FOOD AND HABITS

Food	invertebrates
Nest	grasses, under logs and stones and in burrows
Behaviour	alternately active and resting throughout 24 hours; young 'caravan'
Voice	squeaks
Hibernation	none
Migration	none

LIFE CYCLE

Litters	1 a year; spring–autumn
Young	2–6; naked and helpless
Maturity	probably 2–3 months
Longevity	1–2 years

White-toothed shrews are generally grey-brown and have 'whiskery' tails; they lack any pigment in the teeth. Although the Greater is generally larger than the Lesser White-toothed Shrew (*C. suaveolens*), the only reliable method of separating the two is by their teeth. The Greater's second tooth on the lower jaw has only one cusp, whereas that of the Lesser has two. Both species occur in a wide range of habitats, often close to human habitations.

Range: a wide distribution in western Europe, including many Mediterranean islands and the Channel Islands of Alderney, Guernsey, and Herm.

Similar Species: the Lesser White-toothed Shrew and the Bicoloured White-toothed Shrew (*C. leucodon*), which can only be reliably distinguished by their teeth. Other species also occur in southern Europe.

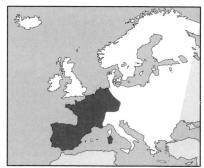

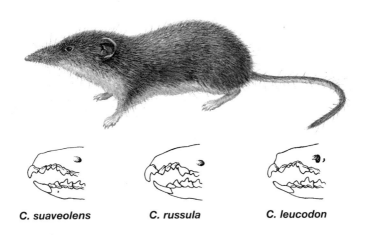

C. suaveolens   **C. russula**   **C. leucodon**

The smallest Crocidura shrew. It is grey to dark brown above, paler below, and the feet are hairy. It occurs in a variety of habitats, and in the Isles of Scilly is often found on the seashore.
Range: a fairly wide distribution in Europe but absent from much of the north and a large part of Iberia. It occurs on all the larger islands in the Isles of Scilly, on Jersey and Sark in the Channel Islands, and on Ouessant and Yeu off the coast of France.
Similar Species: the Bicoloured White-toothed Shrew (*C. leucodon*) has a range that overlaps those of both the Greater (*C. russula*) and Lesser White-toothed Shrews, and is similar in size to the former. It is distinctively coloured with a dark back and pale belly, separated by a clear dividing line along the sides. These shrews are, however, best distinguished by their teeth.

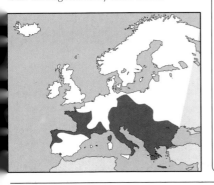

LESSER WHITE-TOOTHED SHREW

Type	shrew
Habitat	very variable; includes gardens, seashore, scrub
Status	not threatened

PHYSICAL DETAILS

Head & Body	4.9–7.8cm
Tail	2.7–5cm
Weight	3–13.3g
Teeth	$\frac{3.1.1.3}{2.0.1.3}$
Colour	grey-brown above, paler below

FOOD AND HABITS

Food	invertebrates
Nest	under logs and stones, in burrows
Behaviour	alternately active and resting throughout 24 hours; young 'caravan'
Voice	squeaks
Hibernation	none
Migration	none

LIFE CYCLE

Litters	1 a year; spring–autumn
Young	2–6; naked and helpless
Maturity	probably 2–3 months
Longevity	1–2 years

Lesser Horseshoe Bat *Rhinolophus hipposideros*

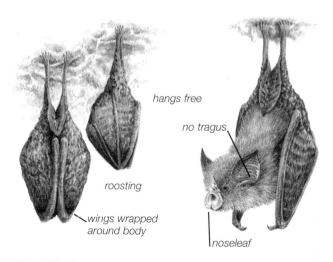

hangs free

no tragus

roosting

wings wrapped around body

noseleaf

LESSER HORSESHOE BAT

Type bat
Habitat mostly woodland; roosts in tunnels, attics, trees
Status endangered throughout most of Europe

PHYSICAL DETAILS

Head & Body 3.7–4.5cm
Tail 2.3–3.3cm
Forearm 3.5–4.25cm
Wingspan 19.2–25.4cm
Weight 3–9g
Teeth $\frac{1.1.2.3}{2.1.3.3}$
Colour dark grey-brown above, paler below

FOOD AND HABITS

Food flying insects, spiders
Nest none
Behaviour nocturnal and crepuscular
Voice ultrasonic; 105–120kHz
Hibernation autumn; in caves, tunnels; 6–9°C
Migration mostly sedentary, but up to 150km

LIFE CYCLE

Litters 1 a year; summer; in nursery colonies of 10–100 females
Young 1; naked and helpless
Maturity 1–2 years
Longevity up to 21 years

The smallest European horseshoe bat, found mostly in woodland habitats. In the north of its range it lives in attics in summer, and hibernates in canal tunnels and cellars. In the south it occurs in caves and mines. The range of its ultrasonic calls overlaps with those of the Mediterranean (*R. euryale*) and Mehely's (*R. mehelyi*) Horseshoe Bats. When roosting it hangs separately, with its wings wrapped around its body.
Range: the most northerly horseshoe bat, found up to latitude 52°, from western Ireland through Wales, England, and continental Europe, north to Luxembourg and east to Russia and the Ukraine. Existing until recently in the southern Netherlands and further north in England, it is now in decline over most of Europe.
Similar Species: other horseshoe bats, all of which are larger.

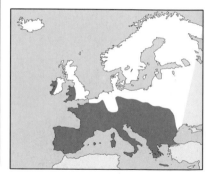

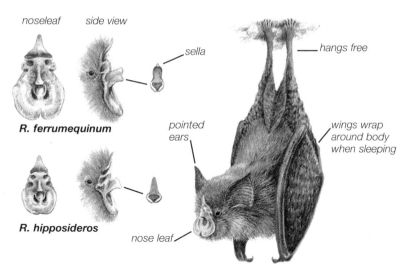

noseleaf

side view

sella

hangs free

R. ferrumequinum

pointed ears

wings wrap around body when sleeping

R. hipposideros

nose leaf

The largest European horseshoe bat. It roosts singly or in large clusters, with its wings wrapped loosely around its body. Caves, attics, cellars and tunnels in areas of open woodland, often near water and in limestone areas, are common roosting places. The Greater Horseshoe Bat has undergone a massive decline, due to changing agricultural practices and indiscriminate use of pesticides. Many roosts have also suffered from disturbance.

Range: formerly widespread over most of western Europe as far north as southern England and Wales, and east to Slovakia and the Balkans. It is now very much reduced over all of its range and almost extinct in Britain.

Similar Species: all other horseshoe bats are smaller.

GREATER HORSESHOE BAT

Type	bat
Habitat	open woodland, pasture
Status	endangered throughout Europe

PHYSICAL DETAILS

Head & Body	5.7–7.1cm
Tail	3.5–4.3cm
Forearm	5.4–6.1cm
Wingspan	33–40cm
Weight	13–34g
Teeth	1.1.2.3
	2.1.3.3
Colour	grey-brown above, white below

FOOD AND HABITS

Food	mostly flying insects, particularly large beetles
Nest	none
Behaviour	nocturnal and crepuscular
Voice	ultrasonic; 77–83kHz
Hibernation	autumn–spring; in caves; 7–10°C
Migration	usually 20–30km, but up to 180km, between winter and summer roosts

LIFE CYCLE

Litters	1 a year; summer; in nursery colonies of up to 200 females
Young	1; naked and helpless
Maturity	2–4 years
Longevity	up to 30 years

Mediterranean Horseshoe Bat *Rhinolophus euryale*

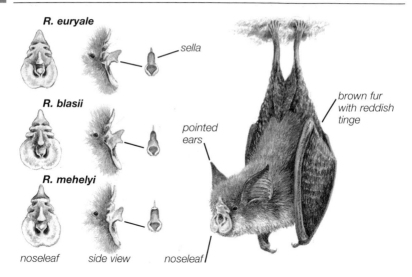

R. euryale

sella

R. blasii

pointed
ears

brown fur
with reddish
tinge

R. mehelyi

noseleaf   side view   noseleaf

	MEDITERRANEAN HORSESHOE BAT	
Type	bat	
Habitat	caves, rock clefts, roofs	
Status	declining and probably endangered	

PHYSICAL DETAILS

Head & Body	4.3–5.8cm	
Tail	2.2–3cm	
Forearm	4.3–5.1cm	
Wingspan	30–32cm	
Weight	8–17.5g	
Teeth	1.1.2.3	
	2.1.3.3	
Colour	grey-brown above, greyish white below	

FOOD AND HABITS

Food	insects, particularly moths
Nest	none
Behaviour	nocturnal and crepuscular
Voice	ultrasonic; 101–108kHz
Hibernation	period unknown; in caves, tunnels; 10°C
Migration	normally sedentary, but up to 134km

LIFE CYCLE

Litters	1 a year; summer; in nursery colonies of up to 400 females
Young	1; naked and helpless
Maturity	in 2nd year
Longevity	about 20 years

A medium-sized horseshoe bat. The upper connecting process of the nose-leaf is pointed, and always longer than the lower process. The Mediterranean Horseshoe Bat has a slow fluttering flight, often hovering, and may hunt in dense foliage. It roosts in caves, attics, and cellars. The nursery colonies are often mixed with other species of bats. When roosting, this bat's wings do not completely envelop its body.
Range: mostly confined to southern Europe, but extends north to northern France and Slovakia. It also occurs on some Mediterranean islands, including Sicily, Corsica and Sardinia.
Similar Species: Blasius's Horseshoe Bat (*R. blasii*) and Mehely's Horseshoe Bat (*R. mehelyi*), both of which can only be distinguished from each other with certainty by the length of the fingers and the shape of the noseleaf.

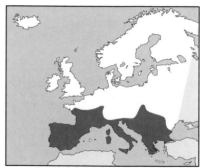

pinkish face

large hind foot

A medium-sized bat with large feet. Often very abundant, it sometimes hibernates in groups of several thousands. It is found mostly in open woodland and parkland, feeding over water. In summer it roosts in attics and trees, often in holes close to the ground. In winter it hibernates underground, usually in crevices, but sometimes hanging free or in clusters. *Range:* much of Europe, but absent from northern Scandinavia, Italy and most of the Balkans. It is found on Sardinia, Corsica, the Balearic Isles, Malta, Sicily and other islands. *Similar Species:* likely to be confused with all other similar sized Myotis bats. The Pond Bat (*M. dasycneme*) is larger; Natterer's Bat (*M. nattereri*) has a hairy edge to the tail membrane and Geoffroy's Bat (*M. emarginatus*) is usually reddish brown.

DAUBENTON'S BAT

Type	bat
Habitat	open woodland, parkland; often hunts over water
Status	moderately abundant; increasing in some areas, declining in others

PHYSICAL DETAILS

Head & Body	4.5–5.5cm
Tail	3.1–4.45cm
Forearm	3.5–4.17cm
Wingspan	24–27.5cm
Weight	7–15g
Teeth	$\frac{2.1.3.3}{3.1.3.3}$
Colour	reddish brown above, grey-white below

FOOD AND HABITS

Food	insects, midges, mayflies
Nest	none
Behaviour	nocturnal and crepuscular
Voice	ultrasonic; 69–25kHz
Hibernation	autumn–early spring; caves and tunnels; 3–6°C, occasionally down to -2°C
Migration	mostly short distances, but up to 240km

LIFE CYCLE

Litters	1 a year; summer; in nursery colonies of up to 200 females (usually 20–50)
Young	1; naked and helpless
Maturity	1 year
Longevity	up to 20 years

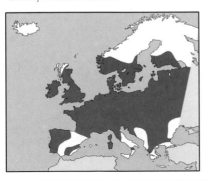

Pond Bat *Myotis dasycneme*

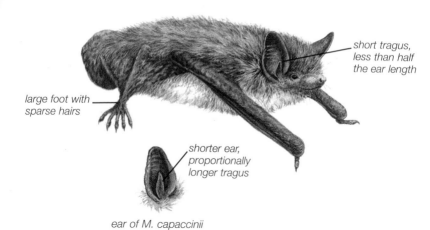

short tragus, less than half the ear length

large foot with sparse hairs

shorter ear, proportionally longer tragus

ear of M. capaccinii

POND BAT

Type bat
Habitat woodland, meadows
Status critically endangered

PHYSICAL DETAILS

Head & Body 5.7–6.8cm
Tail 4.6–5.3cm
Forearm 4.3–4.9cm
Wingspan 20–32cm
Weight 14–20g
Teeth $\frac{2.1.3.3}{3.1.3.3}$
Colour grey-brown above, greyish white below

FOOD AND HABITS

Food insects
Nest none
Behaviour crepuscular and nocturnal
Voice ultrasonic; 60–24kHz
Hibernation autumn–spring; in caves, mines, cellars; 0.5–7.5°C
Migration medium range, irregular migrant, up to 330km

LIFE CYCLE

Litters 1 a year; summer; in nursery colonies of 4–400 females
Young 1; mid-June; naked and helpless
Maturity in 2nd year
Longevity up to 19 years

A medium-sized bat, found in open woodlands and meadows, and often feeding over open water. It roosts in roofs and church towers and hibernates in caves, mines and cellars, hanging singly or in small clusters. This species is seriously endangered, probably as a result of poisoning by chemicals used to treat timber in its nursery colonies. *Range:* confined to central and eastern Europe, from north-eastern France, the Netherlands and Belgium in the east, north to southern Sweden and south to Slovakia.
Similar Species: Daubenton's Bat (*M. daubentonii*) is smaller; the Long-fingered Bat (*M. capaccinii*), is confined to the Mediterranean region. It is smaller than the Pond Bat and has downy hair on the wing membrane, a characteristic ear shape and large feet with obvious bristles.

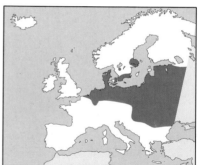

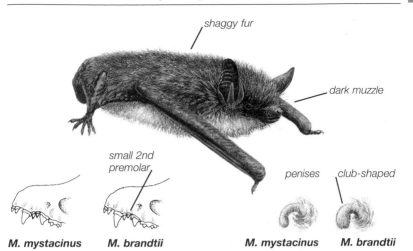

shaggy fur

dark muzzle

small 2nd premolar

M. mystacinus   **M. brandtii**

penises   club-shaped

M. mystacinus   **M. brandtii**

The Whiskered Bat is the smallest of the European Myotis bats. The colouring is variable: dark to light brown above, greyish on the underside. It often hunts over water, and roosts in hollow trees, bird and bat boxes, and attics. In winter it hibernates in caves and tunnels, preferring damp, cold locations.

Range: widespread throughout Europe except the extreme north and much of Iberia. It also occurs on many Mediterranean islands, including Sardinia, Corsica, Sicily and Crete.

Similar Species: other Myotis bats, particularly Brandt's Bat (M. *brandtii*). Although described as long ago as 1845, Brandt's was not differentiated from the Whiskered Bat in Europe until 1958. The two species can be distinguished by their teeth; the male Brandt's also has a distinctive club-shaped penis.

WHISKERED BAT
Type	bat
Habitat	woodland, parkland, gardens
Status	threatened

PHYSICAL DETAILS
Head & Body	3.5–4.8cm
Tail	3–4.3cm
Forearm	3.1–3.7cm
Wingspan	19–22.5cm
Weight	4–8g
Teeth	$\frac{2.1.3.3}{3.1.3.3}$
Colour	dark to light brown above, greyish below

FOOD AND HABITS
Food	flying insects
Nest	none
Behaviour	crepuscular and nocturnal
Voice	ultrasonic; 75–32kHz
Hibernation	autumn–early spring; in caves, tunnels; 2–8°C
Migration	normally sedentary, but up to 240km

LIFE CYCLE
Litters	1 a year; summer; in nursery colonies of 20–70 females
Young	1; mid-June
Maturity	less than 1 year
Longevity	up to 19 years

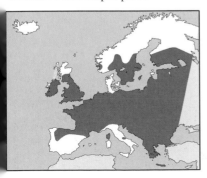

Natterer's Bat *Myotis nattereri*

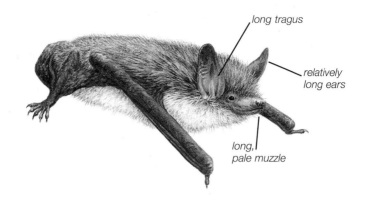

long tragus

relatively long ears

long, pale muzzle

NATTERER'S BAT

Type	bat
Habitat	woodland
Status	endangered in many parts of Europe

PHYSICAL DETAILS

Head & Body	4.2–5.55cm
Tail	3.8–4.7cm
Forearm	3.5–4.3cm
Wingspan	22–30cm
Weight	5–12g
Teeth	2.1.3.3 3.1.3.3
Colour	greyish brown above, white below

FOOD AND HABITS

Food	flying insects
Nest	none
Behaviour	nocturnal and crepuscular
Voice	ultrasonic; 78–35kHz
Hibernation	autumn–spring; in caves, mines; 2.5–8°C
Migration	normally sedentary, but up to 90km

LIFE CYCLE

Litters	1 a year; summer; in nursery colonies of 20–200 females
Young	1; naked and helpless
Maturity	in 2nd year
Longevity	up to 20 years

A medium-sized Myotis bat, with relatively large ears, and white underparts. One of the most distinctive features of Natterer's Bat is the fringe of stiff bristles along the edge of the tail membrane, and the 'S' shaped calcar. This species hibernates in relatively low temperatures, and often squeezes into narrow cracks and under boulders.
Range: found throughout most of Europe, except northern Scandinavia and the Balkans; it also occurs on Sardinia and Corsica.
Similar Species: all other Myotis bats are similar, particularly Geoffroy's Bat (*M. emarginatus*), which has less hair on the tail membrane, and is more reddish brown.

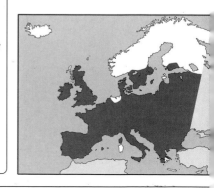

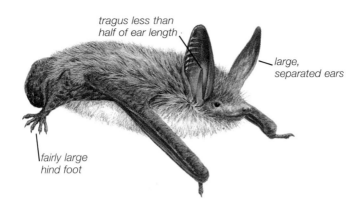

tragus less than half of ear length

large, separated ears

fairly large hind foot

A medium to large, reddish brown bat, with characteristic large, elliptical ears, which extend well beyond the tip of the nose when folded forward. Found in woodland and forest, its scarcity probably reflects the destruction of Europe's primeval forests. It roosts in trees and buildings, hibernating in caves, cellars and tree holes.
Range: central Europe, as far west as France and northern Iberia, south to Italy and Sicily, and east to the western Ukraine and Romania. It also occurs in southern England, where it is very rare.
Similar Species: only likely to be confused with long-eared bats, the ears of which are joined together at the base. All other similar-sized *Myotis* bats have much smaller ears, and the mouse-eared bats are larger.

BECHSTEIN'S BAT

Type	bat
Habitat	forest, woodland
Status	endangered

PHYSICAL DETAILS

Head & Body	4.4–5.5cm
Tail	3–4.5cm
Forearm	3.8–4.7cm
Wingspan	25–30cm
Weight	7–14g
Teeth	$\frac{2.1.3.3}{3.1.3.3}$
Colour	brownish above, pale below

FOOD AND HABITS

Food	insects, often gleaning
Nest	none
Behaviour	nocturnal
Voice	ultrasonic; 80–38kHz
Hibernation	autumn–spring; in caves, mines; 3–7°C
Migration	sedentary

LIFE CYCLE

Litters	1 a year; summer; in nursery colonies of 10–30 females
Young	1; naked and helpless
Maturity	in 2nd year
Longevity	up to 21 years

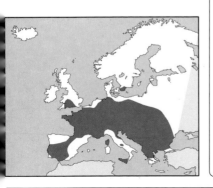

Greater Mouse-eared Bat *Myotis myotis*

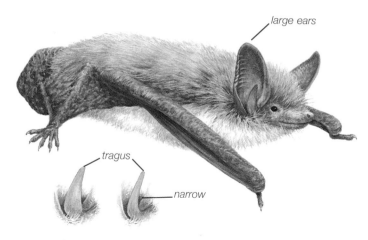

large ears

tragus

narrow

M. myotis   **M. blythii**

GREATER MOUSE-EARED BAT

Type bat
Habitat open woodland, parkland; roosts in buildings in north
Status critically endangered in north of range

PHYSICAL DETAILS

Head & Body 6.7–7.9cm
Tail 4.5–6cm
Forearm 5.4–6.8cm
Wingspan 35–45cm
Weight 26–49g
Teeth 2.1.3.3
3.1.3.3
Colour grey above, whitish below

FOOD AND HABITS

Food insects
Nest none
Behaviour nocturnal
Voice ultrasonic; 105–30kHz
Hibernation autumn–spring; in caves, mines, tunnels; 7–12°C
Migration occasionally up to 390km

LIFE CYCLE

Litters 1 a year; early summer; in nursery colonies of up to 2000 females
Young 1; naked and helpless
Maturity 1 year or more
Longevity up to 22 years

One of the largest bats in Europe with a wingspan of nearly half a metre. The greyish brown fur is thick and short. In the north of its range it occurs in houses and church towers. Elsewhere, it is found in caves and tree holes. It hibernates in caves and cellars, often forming clusters, which once numbered thousands of bats. The population has declined by 80 per cent in Europe. *Range:* widespread over most of Europe as far north as the Netherlands, northern Germany and Poland, with the population in Britain reduced to a single male in the 1990s. It also occurs on Sicily, Sardinia and Corsica. *Similar Species:* the Lesser Mouse-eared Bat (*M. blythii*) is smaller, with a shorter, narrower tragus, and has a more southerly range. However, the two species can often be distinguished only by skull measurements.

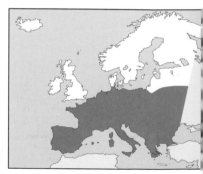

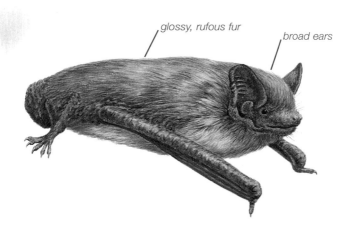

glossy, rufous fur

broad ears

A large bat, with golden-brown fur. The wings are narrow and pointed and the flight is high and fast, with steep dives. The tragus is short and mushroom-shaped. Principally a woodland species, the Noctule Bat often roosts in woodpecker holes. In areas where old trees have been felled and cleared, it is threatened if no alternatives are available. It hibernates in trees, rock clefts, cracks in house walls and, in south-eastern Europe, in caves.
Range: widespread over most of Europe, including many islands, but becoming rare. It is not found in Ireland, northern Scotland or much of Scandinavia.
Similar Species: Leisler's Bat (*N. leisleri*), which is smaller and darker; the Greater Noctule (*N. lasiopterus*), which is much larger. Serotines are darker, and do not have a mushroom-shaped tragus.

NOCTULE BAT
Type	bat
Habitat	woodland, pasture, parkland
Status	declining; endangered

PHYSICAL DETAILS
Head & Body	6–8cm
Tail	4.1–6cm
Forearm	4.7–5.8cm
Wingspan	32–40cm
Weight	19–40g
Teeth	2.1.2.3
	3.1.2.3
Colour	golden-brown

FOOD AND HABITS
Food	large insects
Nest	none
Behaviour	nocturnal and crepuscular
Voice	ultrasonic; 45–25kHz
Hibernation	autumn–early spring; in tree holes, rock clefts, caves; down to 0°C
Migration	up to 930km in Europe

LIFE CYCLE
Litters	1 a year; summer; in nursery colonies of 1 to several hundred females
Young	1–3; naked and helpless
Maturity	1–2 years
Longevity	up to 12 years

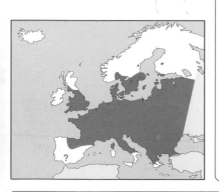

Leisler's Bat *Nyctalus leisleri*

darker and smaller
than N. noctula

rounded tragus

LEISLER'S BAT

Type	bat
Habitat	woodland
Status	rare throughout range

PHYSICAL DETAILS

Head & Body	4.8–6.8cm
Tail	3.5–4.5cm
Forearm	3.8–4.7cm
Wingspan	26–32cm
Weight	11–20g
Teeth	2.1.2.3
	3.1.2.3
Colour	reddish brown above, lighter below

FOOD AND HABITS

Food	insects
Nest	none
Behaviour	nocturnal and crepuscular
Voice	ultrasonic; 45–25kHz
Hibernation	autumn–spring; tree holes, buildings; temperature range unknown
Migration	up to 810km

LIFE CYCLE

Litters	1 a year; summer; in nursery colonies of up to 500 females
Young	1 in west, 2 in east; naked and helpless
Maturity	often in 1st year
Longevity	up to 9 years

A medium-sized bat that is similar to a small noctule, but slightly darker. Inhabiting woodland, it roosts in tree holes and buildings, and occasionally in bat boxes. Its flight is also similar to that of the noctules, being often high and fast, with steep dives.

Range: rather fragmented throughout most of Europe, with populations in Portugal, France and eastward through Italy and central Europe to Russia. It occurs as far south as Greece and Bulgaria and north to England and Wales, and is reasonably widespread in Ireland.

Similar Species: the Noctule Bat (*N. noctula*) and the Greater Noctule Bat (*N. lasiopterus*) are both larger; pipistrelles are all smaller with a forearm that is less than 3.8cm.

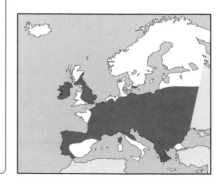

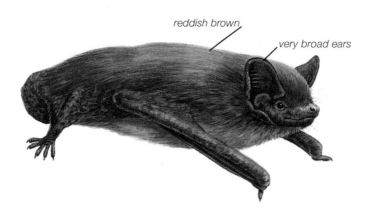

reddish brown

very broad ears

The largest bat in Europe, with a wingspan of nearly half a metre. It is very similar in general appearance to the Noctule Bat (*N. noctula*), but is generally darker, and noticeably larger. It is also one of the least known European bats, with very little data on distribution, habits or behaviour. *Range:* relatively poorly known, and apparently occurring in widely separated, isolated populations. It is most widespread in eastern Europe and Russia, and also west as far as Italy and Switzerland; odd records exist from France and Spain. It also occurs in Sicily and possibly Sardinia, and some other islands in the Tyrrenhian region. *Similar Species:* the Noctule Bat and Leisler's Bat (*N. leisleri*) are both smaller. The only other similar sized bat is the Greater Mouse-eared Bat (*Myotis myotis*), which has large ears.

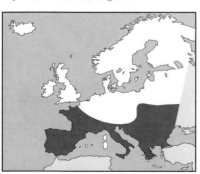

GREATER NOCTULE BAT

Type	bat
Habitat	mostly deciduous woodland
Status	possibly declining

PHYSICAL DETAILS

Head & Body	8.4–10.4cm
Tail	5.5–6.5cm
Forearm	6.3–6.9cm
Wingspan	41–46cm
Weight	41–76g
Teeth	2.1.2.3
	3.1.2.3
Colour	reddish brown above, yellow-brown below

FOOD AND HABITS

Food	insects
Nest	none
Behaviour	nocturnal but little data
Voice	ultrasonic
Hibernation	in tree holes; period and temperature range unknown
Migration	moves southeast for winter

LIFE CYCLE

Litters	1 a year; summer; in nursery colonies of up to 10 females
Young	1 or 2; naked and helpless
Maturity	usually in 2nd year
Longevity	no data

Serotine *Eptesicus serotinus*

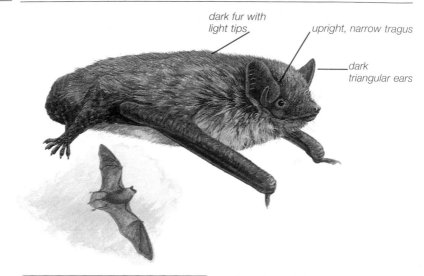

dark fur with light tips

upright, narrow tragus

dark triangular ears

SEROTINE

Type	bat
Habitat	parkland, gardens, wooded farmland
Status	declining; however, range is extending north

PHYSICAL DETAILS

Head & Body	6.2–8.2cm
Tail	3.9–5.9cm
Forearm	4.8–5.7cm
Wingspan	31.5–38cm
Weight	14–33g
Teeth	2.1.1.3 3.1.2.3
Colour	dark brown above, dingy brown below

FOOD AND HABITS

Food	insects
Nest	none
Behaviour	nocturnal and crepuscular
Voice	ultrasonic; 52–25kHz
Hibernation	autumn–spring; in houses, caves; 2–4°C
Migration	mostly sedentary, but up to 330km

LIFE CYCLE

Litters	1 a year; summer; in nursery colonies of up to 100 females
Young	1 (in Europe); naked and helpless
Maturity	less than 1 year
Longevity	at least 19 years

A large bat with long, dark brown fur. Its wings are broad, and it hunts in large loops along hedges, woodland margins and around street lamps, often travelling several kilometres from the roost to its feeding area. Over much of its range the Serotine roosts in houses. In southern Europe it also roosts in caves. Although widespread, it does not occur in large concentrations. Because it lives mainly in buildings this bat is extremely vulnerable to poisoning by chemicals used in timber treatment.
Range: widespread over most of Europe as far north as southern England and Denmark and southern Sweden.
Similar Species: the noctules, which can be distinguished by colouring and the tragus shape; the Northern Bat (*E. nilssonii*) is smaller, and mouse-eared bats are much greyer, with large ears.

yellow-tipped fur

A medium-sized bat, with dark brown fur above, and a paler underside. The fur is yellow-tipped, giving it a glossy sheen. The Northern Bat flies fast, often over water or at tree-top height. It is found in woodland, and roosts in cracks in walls and under roofs. *Range:* widespread in northern and central Europe, from Arctic Scandinavia to northern Italy, Hungary and Romania; in Scandinavia it is often abundant and in some areas even increasing.
Similar Species: Savi's Pipistrelle (*Pipistrellus savii*), which is smaller, and has a more southerly distribution; the Parti-coloured Bat (*Vespertilio murinus*), which has more rounded ears, and 'frosted' fur; the Serotine (*E. serotinus*), which is darker below and larger; Leisler's Bat (*Nyctalus leisleri*), which has a rounded tragus.

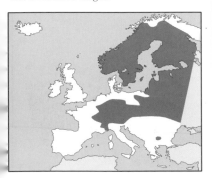

NORTHERN BAT

Type	bat
Habitat	mostly open woodland
Status	little known; vagrant to UK

PHYSICAL DETAILS

Head & Body	4.5–6.4cm
Tail	3.5–5cm
Forearm	3.7–4.4cm
Wingspan	24–28cm
Weight	8–18g
Teeth	2.1.1.3 3.1.2.3
Colour	brown above, with a glossy sheen, paler below

FOOD AND HABITS

Food	insects
Nest	none
Behaviour	nocturnal
Voice	ultrasonic, 38–28kHz
Hibernation	autumn–spring; in caves, tunnels; -5.5–5.5°C
Migration	mostly sedentary, but up to 115km

LIFE CYCLE

Litters	1 a year; summer; in nursery colonies of up to 60 females
Young	1 or 2; naked and helpless
Maturity	no data
Longevity	up to 14.5 years

Parti-coloured Bat *Vespertilio murinus*

white-tipped fur

broad ears

white underside

PARTI-COLOURED BAT	
Type	bat
Habitat	woodland, cliffs, cities
Status	endangered throughout most of range; vagrant to UK

PHYSICAL DETAILS	
Head & Body	4.8–6.4cm
Tail	3.7–4.45cm
Forearm	3.9–4.9cm
Wingspan	27–31cm
Weight	12–20.5g
Teeth	2.1.1.3
	3.1.2.3
Colour	dark brown 'frosted' whitish above, whitish below

FOOD AND HABITS	
Food	insects
Nest	none
Behaviour	nocturnal
Voice	ultrasonic; 50–25kHz; also audible sounds
Hibernation	autumn–early spring; in caves, cellars, usually in crevices; temperature range unknown
Migration	highly migratory; up to 900km in south-westerly direction

LIFE CYCLE	
Litters	1 a year; summer; in nursery colonies of 30–50 females
Young	usually 2, occasionally 3; naked and helpless
Maturity	no data
Longevity	up to 5 years

The dark fur on the back of this medium-sized bat is tipped with white, giving it a 'frosted' appearance. The only other bat with similar fur is the Barbastelle (*Barbastellus barbastellus*), which has a different ear structure. Below, the Parti-coloured Bat is almost white, with a clear line of demarcation from the upper parts. Its original habitat may have been in cliffs and rocky hillsides. More recently, it has adapted to living in tower blocks in cities. Its flight is fast and straight. *Range:* eastern and central Europe as far west as eastern France and Italy, and as far north as southern Scandinavia and Finland. *Similar Species:* the Northern Bat (*Eptesicus nilssonii*), the Serotine (*E. serotinus*) and Leisler's Bat (*Nyctalus leisleri*), all of which lack the 'frosted' fur.

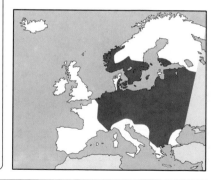

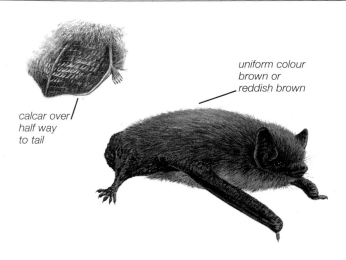

uniform colour
brown or
reddish brown

calcar over
half way
to tail

The smallest European bat, with short, triangular ears. Throughout most of its range it is usually the most common bat, and is frequently found roosting in houses. Hibernating bats hang in clusters numbering up to 10,000 individuals. However, the Common Pipistrelle has undergone massive declines in many areas, largely due to poisoning by chemicals used in treating roof timbers.
Range: widespread over most of Europe, north to southern Scandinavia; also found on most Mediterranean islands.
Similar Species: small *Myotis* bats, all of which have larger, paler ears. Kuhl's (*P. kuhli*) and Savi's (*P. savii*) Pipistrelles are larger; Nathusius's Pipistrelle (*P. nathusii*) has a longer fifth finger, and a hairier tail membrane.

COMMON PIPISTRELLE

Type	bat
Habitat	very varied; almost ubiquitous
Status	most common bat over most of range, but many local declines

PHYSICAL DETAILS

Head & Body	3.2–5.1cm
Tail	2–3.6cm
Forearm	2.8–3.5cm
Wingspan	18–24cm
Weight	3.5–8.5g
Teeth	2.1.2.3 / 3.1.2.3
Colour	brownish above, slightly paler below, with black ears and wings

FOOD AND HABITS

Food	insects
Nest	none
Behaviour	nocturnal and crepuscular
Voice	ultrasonic; 80–58kHz; also audible sounds
Hibernation	autumn–spring; in caves, churches, trees; 0–6°C
Migration	mostly sedentary, but up to 770km

LIFE CYCLE

Litters	1 a year; summer; in nursery colonies of up to 1000 females
Young	1 or 2 (1 in UK); naked and helpless
Maturity	1–2 years
Longevity	up to 16 years

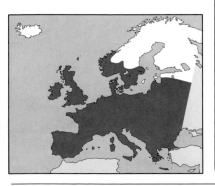

Nathusius's Pipistrelle *Pipistrellus nathusii*

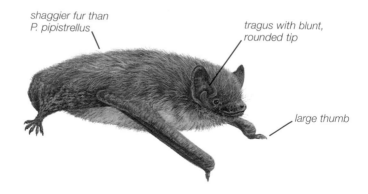

shaggier fur than P. pipistrellus

tragus with blunt, rounded tip

large thumb

NATHUSIUS'S PIPISTRELLE

Type	bat
Habitat	mostly woodland
Status	endangered in west of range

PHYSICAL DETAILS

Head & Body	4.6–5.8cm
Tail	3–4.4cm
Forearm	3.2–3.7cm
Wingspan	22–25cm
Weight	6–15.5g
Teeth	2.1.2.3 / 3.1.2.3
Colour	reddish brown in summer, darker in winter

FOOD AND HABITS

Food	insects
Nest	none
Behaviour	nocturnal and crepuscular
Voice	ultrasonic; 70–38kHz
Hibernation	autumn–spring; crevices, cracks, caves; temperature range unknown
Migration	highly migratory, moving 1000–1600km to south-west in winter

LIFE CYCLE

Litters	1 a year; summer; in nursery colonies of 50–200 females
Young	1 (occasionally 2); naked and helpless
Maturity	1–2 years
Longevity	up to 7 years

A small bat, only slightly larger than the Common Pipistrelle (*P. pipistrellus*). It is reddish or chestnut-brown in summer, moulting into a darker pelage in winter. The tail membrane is hairy on the upper side, and along the legs on the underside. Nathusius's Pipistrelle is a woodland species, and readily adapts to roosting in bat boxes. It sometimes shares roosts with other bats, including the Common Pipistrelle and Brandt's Bat (*M. brandti*).

Range: mostly central and eastern Europe; there may also be populations in Iberia and Scandinavia; there are isolated records from the UK.

Similar Species: Kuhl's (*P. kuhlii*) and Savi's (*P. savii*) Pipistrelles have a more southerly distribution and have short thumbs. Savi's is rather like a small Northern Bat (*Eptesicus nilssonii*).

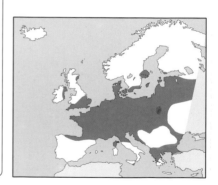

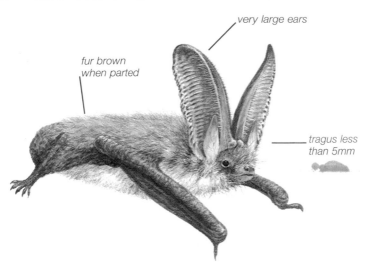

very large ears

fur brown
when parted

tragus less
than 5mm

A medium-sized bat with huge ears. The fur on the underside is brownish when parted. Throughout most of its range the Brown Long-eared Bat is a relatively common species, found mostly in wooded habitats, gardens and parkland, where it feeds with a slow, fluttering and hovering flight. In summer it often roosts in houses, and in winter hibernates in relatively cold places, often near cave entrances.
Range: found in most of Europe except the extreme north, Iberia and south-western France.
Similar Species: the Grey Long-eared Bat (*P. austriacus*), which can be distinguished by its greyish underfur and wider tragus. It has a more southerly distribution, and is very rare in England. Bechstein's Bat (*Myotis bechsteinii*) also has large ears but they are much more widely separated.

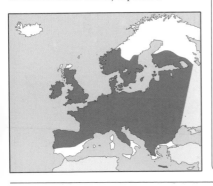

BROWN LONG-EARED BAT

Type	bat
Habitat	woodland, gardens
Status	common, but greatly reduced and locally threatened

PHYSICAL DETAILS

Head & Body	4.2–5.5cm
Tail	3.2–5.5cm
Forearm	3.4–4.2cm
Wingspan	24–28.5cm
Weight	5–12g
Teeth	2.1.2.3 3.1.3.3
Colour	brown above, paler below

FOOD AND HABITS

Food	insects and spiders
Nest	none; roosts in trees, houses
Behaviour	nocturnal and crepuscular
Voice	ultrasonic; 86–26kHz
Hibernation	autumn–early spring; in caves, buildings, cellars; -3.5–5°C
Migration	normally only local

LIFE CYCLE

Litters	1 a year; summer; in nursery colonies of 10–50+ females
Young	1 (occasionally 2); naked and helpless
Maturity	1–2 years
Longevity	usually 4.5 years, up to 22 years

Barbastelle *Barbastellus barbastellus*

very dark fur with pale tips

broad, joined ears

BARBASTELLE	
Type	bat
Habitat	woodland, particularly in mountainous areas
Status	endangered over most of Europe; no breeding colonies known in the British Isles

PHYSICAL DETAILS

Head & Body	4.5–5.8cm
Tail	3.6–5.2cm
Forearm	3.6–4.4cm
Wingspan	26–29cm
Weight	6–13.5g
Teeth	$\frac{2.1.2.3}{3.1.2.3}$
Colour	dark brown 'frosted' white

FOOD AND HABITS

Food	insects
Nest	none
Behaviour	nocturnal and crepuscular
Voice	ultrasonic; 43–28kHz
Hibernation	autumn–spring; in caves, tunnels, trees; -3–5°C
Migration	up to 300km

LIFE CYCLE

Litters	1 a year; summer; in nursery colonies of 10–100 females
Young	1 (occasionally 2); naked and helpless
Maturity	1–2 years
Longevity	up to 23 years

A medium-sized bat, with characteristic large, dark ears, joined together at the base, and long, dark fur tipped with white, giving it a 'frosted' appearance. In summer it is often found roosting in buildings, and in winter it hibernates in cold areas such as around cave entrances. It has also adapted to using bat boxes. The Barbastelle is one of the least known bats in Europe, and is in decline over most of its range.
Range: most widespread in central Europe, north to southern Britain and Scandinavia, and south to northern Spain, Italy, Slovenia, Romania and the Black Sea coast; it also occurs on the islands of Corsica, Sardinia, and Sicily.
Similar Species: not likely to be confused with any other species.

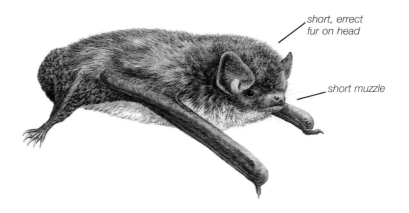

short, erect
fur on head

short muzzle

A medium-sized bat with a very short nose and a high forehead. The short hair on the head stands erect. Schreiber's Bat has long wings and is very fast-flying, having been likened to a swift or swallow. Limestone caves are its preferred habitat, although it is occasionally found in buildings. The northernmost populations migrate south in winter.
Range: confined to southern and eastern Europe. Numbers are declining.
Similar Species: not likely to be confused with any other European species of bat.

SCHREIBER'S BAT
Type bat
Habitat mostly limestone areas
Status extinct or endangered over most of range

PHYSICAL DETAILS
Head & Body 4.8–6.2cm
Tail 4.7–6.4cm
Forearm 4.4–4.8cm
Wingspan 30.5–34.2cm
Weight 9–16g
Teeth 2.1.2.3 / 3.1.3.3
Colour greyish brown above, paler below

FOOD AND HABITS
Food insects
Nest none
Behaviour nocturnal
Voice ultrasonic; also audible whisperings and shrill calls when at rest
Hibernation autumn–early spring; in caves; 7–12°C
Migration in north of range; 100–350km

LIFE CYCLE
Litters 1 a year; summer; in nursery colonies of up to 1000 females
Young 1 (occasionally 2); naked and helpless
Maturity in 2nd year
Longevity 16 years

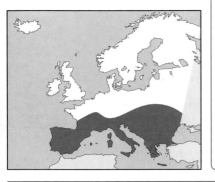

Free-tailed Bat *Tadarida teniotis*

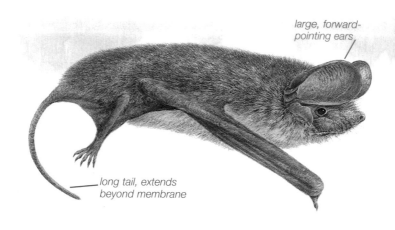

large, forward-pointing ears

long tail, extends beyond membrane

FREE-TAILED BAT

Type	bat
Habitat	rocky hillsides, cliffs, gorges
Status	little known

PHYSICAL DETAILS

Head & Body	8–9.2cm
Tail	4.4–5.7cm
Forearm	5.7–6.5cm
Wingspan	up to 44cm
Weight	25–50g
Teeth	$\frac{1.1.2.3}{3.1.2.3}$
Colour	greyish above, paler below

FOOD AND HABITS

Food	insects
Nest	none
Behaviour	nocturnal and crepuscular
Voice	18–10kHz
Hibernation	unknown
Migration	probably does migrate

LIFE CYCLE

Litters	1 a year; summer
Young	1; naked and helpless
Maturity	about 2 years
Longevity	10+ years

A very large, unmistakable bat with large ears, a long, wrinkled muzzle, and a long tail. The fur is velvety, greyish brown or blackish, and the wings are relatively bony and narrow. It is mostly rock-dwelling, and occurs up to 1920m in the Alps. In summer it occurs in rock clefts and cracks in buildings, but nothing is known of its habits in winter. Its roosts are said to have a musky lavender smell.
Range: confined to Mediterranean Europe, where its distribution is very poorly known.
Similar Species: none in Europe.

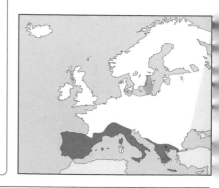

footprints

_ ears shorter than
in L. capensis and
lack black tip

droppings
on anthill

One of the best known and most
frequently observed wild mammals in
Europe, with a characteristic hopping
gait. It is similar to the domestic
varieties, but normally greyish brown.
Tame rabbits often escape and rabbits
with colouration of domestic varieties
occur commonly in the wild. Rabbits
usually excavate extensive burrows
(warrens) in light soils, and graze
around the entrances. The small, round
droppings are characteristic.
Range: originally confined to western
Mediterranean Europe and North
Africa, but introduced extensively
elsewhere. The range now extends to
the British Isles, Corsica, Sicily and
southern Scandinavia. In many areas it
is a major agricultural pest.
Similar Species: hares, which have
longer ears; the Cottontail (*Sylvilagus
floridianus*), which is smaller.

RABBIT	
Type	rabbit
Habitat	grassland, scrub, meadows
Status	common; often pest

PHYSICAL DETAILS	
Head & Body	38–55cm
Tail	4.5–7cm
Weight	1.3–2.5kg
Teeth	2.0.3.3
	1.0.2.3
Colour	greyish brown, white undertail

FOOD AND HABITS	
Food	grass, herbage, bark
Nest	grasses lined with fur, in burrows; occasionally above ground
Behaviour	nocturnal and diurnal
Voice	normally silent
Hibernation	none
Migration	none

LIFE CYCLE	
Litters	up to 5 a year; spring–early autumn
Young	3–8; blind and helpless
Maturity	5–8 months
Longevity	up to 9 years

Brown Hare *Lepus europaeus*

very large,
black-tipped ears

black above

white below

footprints

BROWN HARE

Type	hare
Habitat	open woodland, grassland
Status	not threatened; local declines in England

PHYSICAL DETAILS

Head & Body	50–70cm
Tail	7–11cm
Weight	2.5–7kg
Teeth	2.0.3.3 / 1.0.2.3
Colour	sandy brown above, whitish below

FOOD AND HABITS

Food	grazes and browses on grasses, leaves, shoots, twigs
Nest	none; young born in shallow depression or form
Behaviour	nocturnal and diurnal
Voice	normally silent; loud scream in distress
Hibernation	none
Migration	none, but can move over several kms

LIFE CYCLE

Litters	1–4; late winter onwards
Young	1–5; well developed and active within 1 hour of birth
Maturity	less than 1 year
Longevity	up to 13 years

A large hare weighing up to 7kg. Often conspicuous, it inhabits open fields, steppes, agricultural areas and woodlands. The long, black-tipped ears and the tail, black above, white below, are characteristic.

Range: extensive distribution over most of Europe except northern Scandinavia, and higher altitudes where it is often replaced by the Mountain Hare (L. timidus); it is also absent from Iberia, but occurs on most of the large Mediterranean islands. It was introduced into Ireland in the 19th century.

Similar Species: the African Hare (L. capensis) replaces the Brown Hare in Sardinia. It is smaller, faintly spotted on the nape and has only one young. *L. granatensis* occurs over most of Iberia and in 1977 *L. castroviejoi*, was described from north-western Spain. *L. corsicanus* occurs in southern Italy and Sicily.

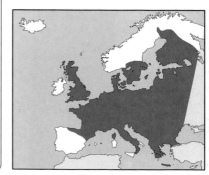

black-tipped ears

winter

summer

footprints

white tail

The Mountain Hare, also known as the Varying or Arctic Hare, is rather more lightly built than the Brown Hare (*L. europaeus*). It is distinguishable from the latter by its all-white tail. Over most of the range it is found in tundra, heathland and montane grasslands. Except in Ireland it turns white in winter. Mountain Hares are sociable and form herds of 40 or more.
Range: extends over most of Scandinavia, the Baltic States, the Alps, the Pyrenees, Scotland and Ireland. It has been introduced into other parts of the British Isles including the Shetland Islands, and the Faroes.
Similar Species: brown hares, which are larger and darker; the Rabbit (*Oryctolagus cuniculus*), which has no black tips to the ears. Hybrids between the Mountain Hare and the European Brown Hare are known.

MOUNTAIN HARE

Type	hare
Habitat	open tundra, heathland, farmland, mountains
Status	not threatened

PHYSICAL DETAILS

Head & Body	46–65cm
Tail	4.3–8cm
Weight	2–6kg
Teeth	2.0.3.3 / 1.0.2.3
Colour	grey-brown in summer, white in winter (except Ireland), with black ear tips

FOOD AND HABITS

Food	heather, grass, willow, birch and other twigs
Nest	short burrows, or depression in ground
Behaviour	nocturnal and diurnal
Voice	normally silent
Hibernation	none
Migration	in mountains moves to lower altitudes in winter

LIFE CYCLE

Litters	2–3 a year; summer
Young	2–5; active soon after birth
Maturity	in 2nd year
Longevity	up to c9 years

Cottontail *Sylvilagus floridianus*

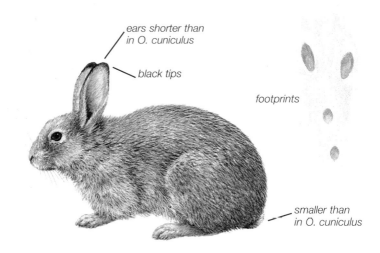

ears shorter than
in *O. cuniculus*

black tips

footprints

smaller than
in *O. cuniculus*

COTTONTAIL

Type	rabbit
Habitat	scrub, thickets, agricultural land
Status	introduced; potential pest

PHYSICAL DETAILS

Head & Body	35–43cm
Tail	4–6.5cm
Weight	0.9–1.8kg
Teeth	$\frac{2.0.3.3}{1.0.2.3}$
Colour	greyish brown, with black flecks, and reddish brown nape

FOOD AND HABITS

Food	grasses, herbs
Nest	grasses and fur in shallow depression, usually in dense scrub, or thick grass
Behaviour	nocturnal and diurnal
Voice	usually silent
Hibernation	none
Migration	none

LIFE CYCLE

Litters	3–4 a year; summer
Young	usually 4–5, up to 9; naked and blind
Maturity	6–8 weeks
Longevity	generally less than 1 year

A small rabbit with shorter ears than the European Rabbit (*Oryctolagus cuniculus*). It is greyish brown with a noticeable reddish brown patch on the nape and often a white patch between the ears. As in the Rabbit the underside of its tail (scut) is white.

Range: a North American species introduced into Europe, from about 1953 onwards. It is well established in southern France and northern Italy, and is apparently spreading but its range is not well known.

Similar Species: most likely to be confused with the Rabbit, which is larger. The New England Cottontail (*S. transitionalis*) was introduced into Germany in the 1980s. It is very similar to the Cottontail but has a black patch between the ears. At present, the ranges do not overlap.

Sciurus vulgaris # Red Squirrel

ear tufts
(in winter)

gnawed
hazel nut

dark form

red form

tail bleaches
in some areas

The only squirrel that occurs throughout most of Europe. The colouring is variable, ranging from light red (the tail fades to almost white in some areas), through bright chestnut red, to almost jet black. In winter the ears have prominent tufts. The Red Squirrel is an agile climber and is found in a variety of wooded habitats.
Range: widespread over most of mainland Europe but absent from most of southern and western Iberia, and from most Mediterranean islands. Nearly extinct in England, but it is still abundant in Scotland and Ireland.
Similar Species: the closely related Persian Squirrel (*S. anomalus*) occurs on the Greek island of Lesbos and around Istanbul. It is superficially similar, but slightly smaller and has one fewer upper premolar. See also the Grey Squirrel.

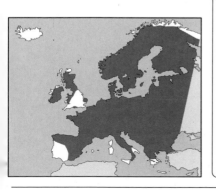

RED SQUIRREL

Type	squirrel
Habitat	woodland, forest, parkland
Status	endangered in England; often abundant elsewhere

PHYSICAL DETAILS

Head & Body	18–27cm
Tail	14–20cm
Weight	200–480g
Teeth	$\frac{1.0.2.3}{1.0.1.3}$
Colour	variable; bright reddish brown to black above, whitish below

FOOD AND HABITS

Food	shoots, nuts, pine cones, fungi, birds' eggs
Nest	bulky ball of twigs and leaves, close to trunk of tree
Behaviour	diurnal
Voice	regular, scolding 'chuk-chuk-chuk'
Hibernation	none; stays within nest in severe weather
Migration	none

LIFE CYCLE

Litters	2 a year; late winter–early summer
Young	3–7; blind and helpless
Maturity	from 6 months; normally 10–12 months
Longevity	5–10 years

Grey Squirrel *Sciurus carolinensis*

lacks
ear tufts

grey, rust-brown
and whitish tail

stripped
pine cone

GREY SQUIRREL	
Type	squirrel
Habitat	woodland, parkland, gardens
Status	common; occasionally a pest

PHYSICAL DETAILS	
Head & Body	23–30cm
Tail	14–24cm
Weight	400–800g
Teeth	$\frac{1.0.2.3}{1.0.1.3}$
Colour	grey, sometimes tinged brown above, paler below

FOOD AND HABITS	
Food	seeds, nuts, berries, shoots, buds; also insects, birds' eggs
Nest	bulky ball of leaves; also in tree holes and roofs
Behaviour	diurnal
Voice	chattering and scolding calls
Hibernation	none; may stay within nest during bad weather
Migration	none

LIFE CYCLE	
Litters	2 a year; late winter, summer
Young	1–7; blind and helpless
Maturity	6–12 months
Longevity	8–9 years

Larger and more adaptable than the native Red Squirrel (*S. vulgaris*), the Grey has largely replaced that species in England and Wales since introductions began in the 19th century. Although occasionally tinged russet, the fur is essentially grey, and unlike the Red this squirrel never has ear tufts. The tail is grey with almost black hairs and a whitish edge. The drey is built from leaves and twigs; this species also nests in tree holes and roofs. Nuts are stored in autumn.

Range: introduced into the British Isles from North America at about 30 sites between 1876 and 1929, and thence to Ireland in 1913. It is now widespread and often abundant in England and Wales, and the range is still spreading in Scotland and Ireland.

Similar Species: the Red Squirrel – see above.

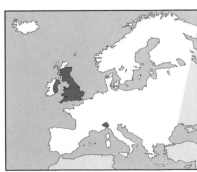

large eyes

'flying' membrane

A small squirrel with large eyes and soft, silvery grey fur. Its most distinctive feature is the flight membrane, which stretches along the flanks between the fore and hind limbs. Using this the squirrel can glide between trees, and change direction, although it cannot truly fly. The Flying Squirrel spends the day in its nest in an old woodpecker hole, and only emerges in darkness. *Range:* extends from the Baltic states and Finland eastwards across Siberia. It is probably declining, due to the clearance of older trees.
Similar Species: the Edible Dormouse (*Glis glis*) is very similar in size and appearance, although it lacks the flight membrane. It may occur in the south of the Flying Squirrel's range.

FLYING SQUIRREL

Type	squirrel
Habitat	mature northern forests
Status	declining in Europe

PHYSICAL DETAILS

Head & Body	13.5–20.5cm
Tail	9–14cm
Weight	90–170g
Teeth	1.0.0.3 / 1.0.0.3
Colour	silvery grey above, whitish below

FOOD AND HABITS

Food	shoots, buds, seeds, nuts, berries
Nest	in old woodpecker holes
Behaviour	strictly nocturnal
Voice	unknown
Hibernation	none; may stay within nest hole in winter and feed on abundant stored food
Migration	none

LIFE CYCLE

Litters	2 a year; spring–summer
Young	2–4; blind and helpless
Maturity	in 2nd year
Longevity	no data

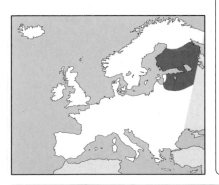

European Souslik *Spermophilus citellus*

small ears

slender, furred tail

	EUROPEAN SOUSLIK
Type	squirrel
Habitat	open steppes, scrub
Status	declining
	PHYSICAL DETAILS
Head & Body	17.5–24cm
Tail	4–8cm
Weight	200–340g
Teeth	1.0.2.3
	1.0.1.3
Colour	sandy brown
	FOOD AND HABITS
Food	herbage, seed, insects
Nest	in colonial burrows
Behaviour	diurnal; colonial
Voice	normally silent
Hibernation	in burrows plugged with grasses and earth; late summer–spring
Migration	none
	LIFE CYCLE
Litters	1 a year; spring–early summer
Young	3–8; blind and helpless
Maturity	year following birth
Longevity	up to 8 years in captivity, less in wild

A ground squirrel that lives in colonies, often around agricultural lands, as well as on steppes and pastures. It digs burrows, and only occurs in areas with suitable light soils.

Range: extends from southern Poland and eastern Germany, south to northern Greece. In recent years it has declined in many areas, probably due to intensification of agriculture.

Similar Species: the Spotted Souslik (*S. suslicus*) is similar in shape and appearance but has white spotting on its back; it is confined to eastern Europe in steppe habitats and arable lands. The Siberian Chipmunk (*Eutamias sibiricus*) is a much smaller ground squirrel, with black and white stripes on its back. It has been introduced into France, Germany, Austria and the Netherlands.

small ears

short, bushy tail

A large, heavily built ground squirrel, living in colonies in alpine regions. The whistling noise it makes is a characteristic sound of the high Alps. In the morning it emerges from burrows to sunbathe, and in summer makes haystacks, which it stores to eat in winter.

Range: the Alpine Marmot is naturally confined to the Alps and the Tatras. During the 1950s it was established in the Pyrenees and in the 1970s was introduced into the Massif Central in France. Since the 1880s there have been many translocations and reintroductions of this species within the Alps and former Yugoslavia.

Similar Species: the only other marmot to have occurred in Europe was the Bobak Marmot (*M. bobak*), which was once found in steppe areas of eastern Europe, but is now extinct.

ALPINE MARMOT

Type	squirrel
Habitat	mountain meadows
Status	not threatened

PHYSICAL DETAILS

Head & Body	40–60cm
Tail	13–20cm
Weight	3–8kg
Teeth	1.0.2.3
	1.0.1.3
Colour	brownish, tail darker

FOOD AND HABITS

Food	mostly grasses, herbage
Nest	in burrows, among rocks
Behaviour	diurnal; colonial
Voice	distinctive whistle
Hibernation	autumn–spring; in nest
Migration	none

LIFE CYCLE

Litters	1 a year; summer
Young	2–6; blind and helpless
Maturity	year following birth
Longevity	up to 20 years

European Beaver *Castor fiber*

flattened, scaly tail

beaver lodge

tree stump left by beaver

EUROPEAN BEAVER

Type	beaver
Habitat	rivers, lakes, swamps
Status	once endangered; recovering

PHYSICAL DETAILS

Head & Body	75–100cm
Tail	30–40cm
Weight	23–35kg
Teeth	$\frac{1.0.1.3}{1.0.1.3}$
Colour	glossy blackish brown

FOOD AND HABITS

Food	aquatic vegetation, shoots, twigs
Nest	lodges and burrows
Behaviour	nocturnal and diurnal; lives in small colonies
Voice	normally silent; slaps tail on water
Hibernation	none
Migration	none

LIFE CYCLE

Litters	1 a year; summer
Young	2–6; fully furred and active soon after birth
Maturity	in 3rd year
Longevity	up to 17 years

The European Beaver is the largest rodent in Europe, and is unlikely to be mistaken for any other species. It has a broad, flattened tail, and large orange incisors.

Range: once occurred throughout most of Europe but by the early 19th century extinct apart from the Rhone in France and the Elbe in northern Poland. It is now protected and, as a result of reintroductions, occurs more widely in Norway, Sweden, the Baltic republics, Germany, Switzerland and France. Experimental reintroductions are taking place in Scotland and England.

Similar Species: the introduced Muskrat (*Ondatra zibethicus*) and Coypu (*Myocastor coypus*), both of which have long, thin tails. The North American Beaver (*C. canadensis*) has been introduced to Finland and the USSR. It is indistinguishable in the field.

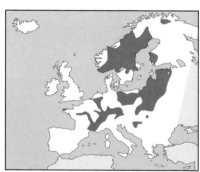

long spines

A large, unmistakable rodent, with long spiny black and white quills. The quills are only loosely attached and easily fall out if touched. The Porcupine occurs in scrubland, rocky hillsides and agricultural areas, digging extensive burrows, often among rocks.

Range: this species is probably not native to Europe, but was introduced during Roman times from North Africa, where it was once widespread. It may have occurred on the Adriatic coast from Croatia south to Greece, but there is no recent evidence for this. Apparently, it is still found in Italy and Sicily, where it is locally abundant.

Similar Species: the only other European mammals with spines are hedgehogs, which are much smaller.

PORCUPINE

Type	porcupine
Habitat	arid rocky areas
Status	locally abundant

PHYSICAL DETAILS

Head & Body	60–80cm
Tail	5–9cm
Weight	15–30kg
Teeth	1.0.1.3
	1.0.1.3
Colour	mostly blackish and grey

FOOD AND HABITS

Food	roots, bulbs, twigs, bark, other plant matter
Nest	in burrows or among rocks
Behaviour	nocturnal
Voice	growls, while rattling spines
Hibernation	none, but often inactive in winter
Migration	none

LIFE CYCLE

Litters	1–3 a year; summer
Young	1–4; with short, soft spines
Maturity	in 2nd year
Longevity	up to 20 years

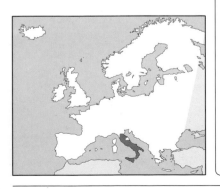

Garden Dormouse *Eliomys quercinus*

black
face
mask

tip of tail
black above,
white below

GARDEN DORMOUSE

Type	dormouse
Habitat	woodland, orchards, scrub
Status	not threatened

PHYSICAL DETAILS

Head & Body	10–18cm
Tail	9–13cm
Weight	50–180g
Teeth	$\frac{1.0.1.3}{1.0.1.3}$
Colour	brown above, white below; black face mask

FOOD AND HABITS

Food	invertebrates, nestling birds, mammals; in autumn, fruits, berries, seeds, nuts, etc.
Nest	usually close to ground
Behaviour	nocturnal
Voice	squeaks, chatters
Hibernation	autumn–spring; in underground burrows, tree holes
Migration	none

LIFE CYCLE

Litters	1 or 2 a year; summer
Young	2–9; blind and helpless
Maturity	in 2nd year
Longevity	5 years

The Garden or Oak Dormouse has a distinctive black mask, and a long, furry tail, tipped black and white. The fur is sandy brown above, white below. It is found mostly in woodland, parkland, orchards and gardens. Although an agile climber, it often forages on the ground. Its nest of leaves and twigs is usually built close to the ground, often among rocks or in drystone walls. Winter nests for hibernation are more sheltered.
Range: widespread in western Europe, extending eastwards through central Europe to Romania and the USSR, and south to Iberia, Italy and several Mediterranean islands, including Sicily, Corsica, Sardinia, and the Balearics.
Similar Species: the Forest Dormouse (*Dryomys nitedula*), which is smaller and has no black on its tail, and much less on its face.

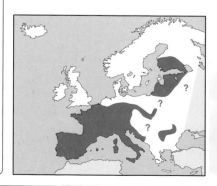

black face mask

bushy tail

In its general appearance the Forest Dormouse is like a smaller version of the Garden Dormouse (*Eliomys quercinus*), with less black colouring. It has a furry tail and is an agile climber. Like the Garden Dormouse it eats insects and other animal life, but is generally more vegetarian. The summer nest is a ball of grasses, usually in a hole, a nest box, or an underground burrow; the winter nest is often underground, and can be up to 60cm below the surface. The Forest Dormouse is mainly found in dense forest, and hibernates only in the north.

Range: extends from central Europe as far north as Poland and Germany, south to Greece and east to Asia.

Similar Species: the Garden Dormouse, which has more black on its face and tail; the Hazel Dormouse (*Muscardinus avellanarius*), which is more orange.

FOREST DORMOUSE

Type	dormouse
Habitat	woodland with thick undergrowth
Status	not threatened

PHYSICAL DETAILS

Head & Body	7.7–11cm
Tail	6–9.5cm
Weight	17–32g
Teeth	$\frac{1.0.1.3}{1.0.1.3}$
Colour	sandy brown above, whitish below, black around eyes

FOOD AND HABITS

Food	omnivorous; insects, fruit, seeds, nuts, shoots
Nest	ball of grasses, usually in hole
Behaviour	nocturnal
Voice	unknown
Hibernation	only in north of range; autumn–spring; in underground burrows, tree holes
Migration	none

LIFE CYCLE

Litters	1 or 2 a year; summer
Young	2–6; blind and helpless
Maturity	in 2nd year
Longevity	4 years

Edible Dormouse *Glis glis*

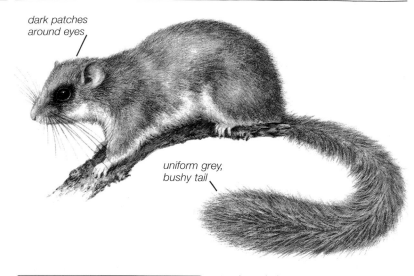

dark patches around eyes

uniform grey, bushy tail

EDIBLE DORMOUSE

Type	dormouse
Habitat	woodland, scrub, gardens, orchards, vineyards
Status	not threatened

PHYSICAL DETAILS

Head & Body	12–20cm
Tail	11–19cm
Weight	70–250g
Teeth	$\frac{1.0.1.3}{1.0.1.3}$
Colour	grey

FOOD AND HABITS

Food	omnivorous; insects, seeds, fruit
Nest	usually in holes; also in nest boxes
Behaviour	nocturnal
Voice	squeaking, snuffling
Hibernation	autumn–spring; in nest
Migration	none

LIFE CYCLE

Litters	1 a year; summer
Young	2–7; blind and helpless
Maturity	after 2nd winter
Longevity	up to 9 years

A relatively large, grey dormouse with a particularly bushy tail, making it look like a miniature squirrel. It is often found in orchards and gardens and may enter houses or sheds, particularly in autumn and winter, when it can be noisy. This species was eaten by the Romans as a delicacy, hence the common name. It becomes very fat before hibernating in holes and attics. *Range:* extends from northern Iberia to the USSR, and south to Italy and Greece. It occurs on Sicily, Corsica, Sardinia, Crete, and has been introduced into England (around Hertfordshire).
Similar Species: the Mouse-tailed Dormouse (*Myomimus roachi*) is similar in colouration, but has a long, slender, short-haired tail, and is smaller. It is confined to a small area of south-eastern Europe and little is known about it.

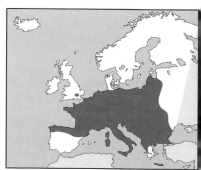

gnawed nut

rich orange-brown

thickly furred tail

nest

A small, bright orange-brown dormouse with a furry tail. Being strictly nocturnal, it is very rarely encountered. The Hazel Dormouse usually occurs in dense vegetation, where it is an agile climber. It is most abundant in deciduous woodland with secondary growth, such as is found in coppiced woodland. The nests are usually close to ground level, and often incorporate shredded honeysuckle bark. This species was once popular as a pet.
Range: widespread over most of western Europe, from France to the USSR, north as far as southern Sweden and southern England and Wales, and reaching south to Italy, Sicily and Greece. In Britain its range appears to have contracted southwards.
Similar Species: no other similarly coloured rodent has a furry tail.

HAZEL DORMOUSE
Type	dormouse
Habitat	woodland
Status	locally rare, but not threatened

PHYSICAL DETAILS
Head & Body	6–8.5cm
Tail	5.5–8cm
Weight	15–43g
Teeth	$\frac{1.0.1.3}{1.0.1.3}$
Colour	bright orange-brown

FOOD AND HABITS
Food	omnivorous; seeds, nuts, insects
Nest	ball of grasses, honeysuckle bark, close to the ground
Behaviour	nocturnal
Voice	occasionally squeaks; may wheeze in hibernation
Hibernation	autumn–spring; underground or in holes, nestboxes
Migration	none

LIFE CYCLE
Litters	1 or 2; summer
Young	3–5; blind and helpless
Maturity	year following birth
Longevity	up to 5 years

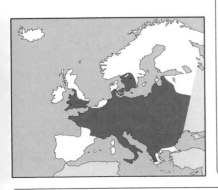

Common Hamster *Cricetus cricetus*

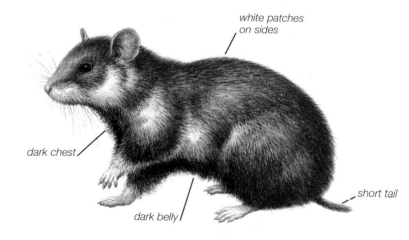

white patches on sides

dark chest

dark belly

short tail

COMMON HAMSTER	
Type	vole
Habitat	steppes, farmland
Status	endangered; locally considered a pest

PHYSICAL DETAILS
Head & Body	22–34cm
Tail	2.8–6cm
Weight	150–600g
Teeth	1.0.0.3 1.0.0.3
Colour	yellowish and reddish brown above, black below

FOOD AND HABITS
Food	omnivorous; seeds, roots, invertebrates
Nest	leaves or grasses, in burrow
Behaviour	nocturnal and crepuscular
Voice	normally silent
Hibernation	autumn–spring; in nest
Migration	occasional, caused by population explosions

LIFE CYCLE
Litters	up to 3 a year; spring–autumn
Young	3–15; naked and helpless
Maturity	c10 weeks
Longevity	up to 3.5 years

A large rodent with a short tail. It is variable in colour, but usually yellowish brown on the back, reddish brown on the head; the sides, muzzle and paws are white, and the belly is black. Occasionally it is entirely black with a white muzzle and white paws. The Common Hamster lives in colonies, and stores food in burrows. It carries food in its cheek pouches, which it inflates if cornered. When disturbed it can jump up to a metre high.

Range: originally confined to the east European steppes, it spread westwards with the clearing of forests, but more recently has declined.

Similar Species: the Romanian Hamster (*Mesocricetus newtoni*), which is smaller, with a white belly; the Guinea Pig (*Cavia porcellus*), which is diurnal, often vocal and does not normally have a black belly.

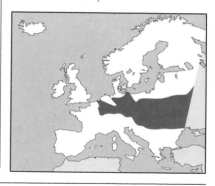

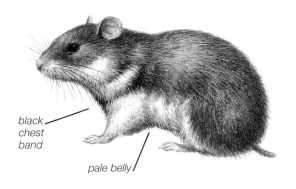

black chest band

pale belly

A short-bodied rodent with a very short tail, like a smaller version of the Common Hamster (*Cricetus cricetus*), but with no black on the belly. The Romanian Hamster occurs in similar agricultural and steppe habitats, where it lives colonially. It feeds on crops, seeds and roots, as well as insect grubs and other invertebrates.

Range: in Europe it occurs only in a small area of Bulgaria, Romania and in Moldavia, along the Black Sea coast.

Similar Species: the Common Hamster, which is much larger with a black belly. The Golden Hamster (*Mesocricetus auratus*) is a very closely related domesticated form that has occasionally become established in small feral populations; most domesticated forms lack the black markings, vary widely in colour and usually have very soft fur.

ROMANIAN HAMSTER

Type	vole
Habitat	steppes, farmland
Status	localized

PHYSICAL DETAILS

Head & Body	10–16cm
Tail	1–1.3cm
Weight	60–150g
Teeth	$\frac{1.0.0.3}{1.0.0.3}$
Colour	sandy brown above, white below, with black on the neck

FOOD AND HABITS

Food	omnivorous; seeds, roots, insects
Nest	in burrows
Behaviour	nocturnal
Voice	normally silent
Hibernation	autumn–early spring; in nest
Migration	none

LIFE CYCLE

Litters	2 a year; summer–early autumn
Young	6–14; naked and helpless
Maturity	no data
Longevity	no data

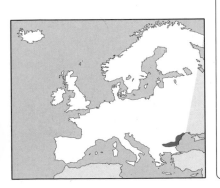

Grey Hamster · *Cricetulus migratorius*

relatively large ears

very short tail

GREY HAMSTER

Type	vole
Habitat	open grassland
Status	localized

PHYSICAL DETAILS

Head & Body	8.7–12cm
Tail	2–3cm
Weight	25–36g
Teeth	$\frac{1.0.0.3}{1.0.0.3}$
Colour	grey-brown above, white below

FOOD AND HABITS

Food	plant matter
Nest	in burrows
Behaviour	mostly nocturnal
Voice	not recorded
Hibernation	none
Migration	often moves in to human habitations in winter

LIFE CYCLE

Litters	up to 3 a year; summer
Young	3–10; naked and helpless
Maturity	no data
Longevity	no data

A small, grey, vole-like hamster. The ears and eyes are larger than in most voles, and the tail is shorter. Unlike other hamsters it is solitary, with each hamster excavating its own burrow. The Grey Hamster is exclusively vegetarian and feeds on a wide variety of plant material, including nuts and seeds. Like other hamsters it stores food for winter, though it does not hibernate. It is also known as the Armenian hamster and has been bred in captivity since 1949.

Range: widespread in Asia, and on the edge of its range in Europe, where it occurs sporadically from the southern Ukraine to Greece and European Turkey.

Similar Species: voles, which have longer tails and smaller ears.

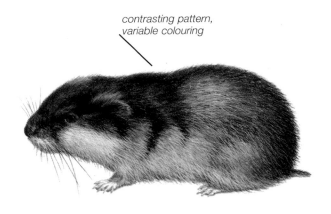

contrasting pattern,
variable colouring

A distinctively coloured, large, vole-like rodent. The strong colouring may be a warning as it is apparently distasteful to predators. If conditions are favourable it is remarkably fecund and Norway Lemmings undergo marked fluctuations in numbers. When the population reaches 100–250 per hectare, emigration takes place. Many animals die on these migrations, which cross rivers and lakes, and may extend the range 200km or more southwards. When the snows melt the ball-shaped winter nests are exposed on the ground. *Range:* confined to the sub-alpine zone of mountain tundra of Scandinavia, extending eastwards as far as the Kola Peninsula in Russia.
Similar Species: not likely to be confused with any other species within its range.

NORWAY LEMMING

Type	vole
Habitat	mountain tundra
Status	not threatened

PHYSICAL DETAILS

Head & Body	13–15cm
Tail	1.5–2cm
Weight	35–130g
Teeth	$\frac{1.0.0.3}{1.0.0.3}$
Colour	very variable; black, white, browns and orange-yellow

FOOD AND HABITS

Food	mosses, grasses, sedges
Nest	in tunnels or beneath snow
Behaviour	nocturnal and diurnal
Voice	hisses, squeaks
Hibernation	none
Migration	explosive migrations in times of overpopulation

LIFE CYCLE

Litters	up to 4 (possibly more) a year, usually 2; summer
Young	2–13; naked and helpless
Maturity	females 20 days, males later
Longevity	up to 4 years

Wood Lemming *Myopus schisticolor*

dark

rufous

very short tail

	WOOD LEMMING
Type	vole
Habitat	coniferous forest
Status	not threatened

PHYSICAL DETAILS

Head & Body	8.5–12.5cm
Tail	1–2cm
Weight	15–45g
Teeth	1.0.0.3
	1.0.0.3
Colour	dark grey with a rufous tinge on the back

FOOD AND HABITS

Food	mosses, lichens
Nest	grasses, in tunnels
Behaviour	both nocturnal and diurnal
Voice	not recorded
Hibernation	none
Migration	similar to Norway Lemming, but less frequent

LIFE CYCLE

Litters	1–3 a year; summer
Young	3–8; naked and helpless
Maturity	20 days
Longevity	probably less than 2 years

A vole-like rodent, easily confused with true voles, but with a very short tail. It mostly occurs in coniferous forest, in areas overgrown with sphagnum moss. The most remarkable feature of its breeding habits is that due to a mutation some females apparently give birth only to females.

Range: relatively little is known about this species; it was thought to have occurred only in isolated populations, but is now known to be fairly widespread from south-eastern Norway to Finland and Russia.

Similar Species: the Red-backed Vole (*Clethrionomys rutilus*), which is more rufous on the back, paler below and has a longer tail; the Grey-sided Vole (*C. rufocanus*) also has a longer tail and is paler below.

upper molars

lower molars

The Bank Vole is reddish brown above, merging into grey along the sides; the belly is pale greyish or greyish yellow. The ears are moderately prominent. It occurs in a wide range of habitats but particularly in hedgerows, forest and woodland. The Bank Vole is an agile climber and also digs its own runs and burrows in the soil and among roots. The nests are often made under logs. *Range:* widespread in Europe, occuring from northern Iberia eastward to Russia and the Ukraine, south to Italy and Greece, and north to Britain and Scandinavia. It is found on some islands around Britain, and also occurs in Ireland, probably as a result of introduction. *Similar Species:* the Red-backed Vole (*C. rutilus*), which has a proportionally shorter tail; the Grey-sided Vole (*C. rufocanus*), which is less rufous.

BANK VOLE

Type	vole
Habitat	woodland, forest, cultivated areas
Status	not threatened; often abundant

PHYSICAL DETAILS

Head & Body	8–12cm
Tail	3–6.5cm
Weight	10–40g
Teeth	$\frac{1.0.0.3}{1.0.0.3}$
Colour	chestnut above, grey below

FOOD AND HABITS

Food	wide range of plant matter, including seeds, berries, nuts, shoots, roots and occasionally also invertebrates
Nest	grasses, leaves, often under logs
Behaviour	nocturnal and diurnal
Voice	chattering, squeaking, also ultrasonic sounds
Hibernation	none
Migration	none

LIFE CYCLE

Litters	up to 4 a year; summer
Young	3–6; naked and helpless
Maturity	from 4.5 weeks
Longevity	up to 3 years

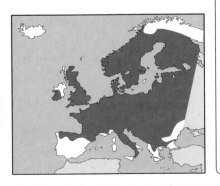

Red-backed Vole *Clethrionomys rutilus*

fairly bright reddish brown

short tail

upper molars

lower molars

molar teeth

Clethrionomys Microtus

	RED-BACKED VOLE
Type	vole
Habitat	tundra, woodland, forest
Status	not threatened

	PHYSICAL DETAILS
Head & Body	8–11cm
Tail	2.3–3.5cm
Weight	15–40g
Teeth	1.0.0.3 / 1.0.0.3
Colour	light rufous above, whitish grey below

	FOOD AND HABITS
Food	seeds, berries, other plant matter
Nest	in burrows
Behaviour	nocturnal and diurnal
Voice	unknown
Hibernation	none
Migration	none

	LIFE CYCLE
Litters	3–4 a year; summer
Young	7–8; naked and helpless
Maturity	probably less than 3 months
Longevity	probably 2–3 years

The Red-backed Vole is very similar to the related Bank Vole (*C. glareolus*), and can be distinguished by its shorter tail and lighter colouring. An agile climber, it often feeds in bushes and trees. In winter it sometimes enters houses. The skulls of *Clethrionomys* species can be distinguished from those of *Microtus* voles by their teeth. The former have separate roots, the latter continuous roots.

Range: in Europe, it is mostly found in the birch woodland of northern Scandinavia, extending southward into coniferous forests.

Similar Species: the Bank Vole – see above; Grey-sided Vole (*C. rufocanus*), which has a more southerly range in Scandinavia, and has the rufous fur confined to the middle of its back; the Wood Lemming (*Myopus schisticolor*) is darker grey.

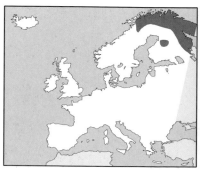

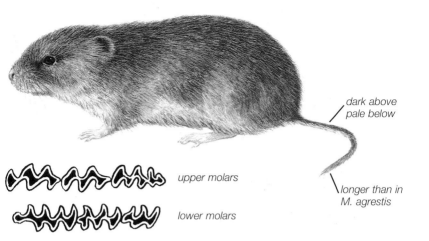

dark above
pale below

upper molars

lower molars

longer than in
M. agrestis

A circumpolar species occurring across Europe, Asia and Alaska. The Root Vole occurs in grassland habitats, including tundra and taiga, and is often found in wetter habitats than other voles. In wet habitats it usually digs tunnels, but may also build grass-lined nests above ground.

Range: wide but discontinuous distribution in Europe, extending over much of north-eastern Europe and northern Scandinavia. Isolated populations occur in the Netherlands and Hungary and some of these are declining.

Similar Species: the Field Vole (*M. agrestis*) is very similar but paler, with shorter fur; the Common Vole (*M. aralis*) is smaller; *Clethrionomys* voles are ruddier.

ROOT VOLE

Type	vole
Habitat	grassland
Status	isolated in south and west; possibly threatened

PHYSICAL DETAILS

Head & Body	9.8–14cm
Tail	3.8–7.4cm
Weight	20–60g
Teeth	$\frac{1.0.0.3}{1.0.0.3}$
Colour	grey

FOOD AND HABITS

Food	roots, grasses, etc.
Nest	grasses, often above ground
Behaviour	nocturnal and diurnal
Voice	squeaks, but normally silent
Hibernation	none
Migration	none

LIFE CYCLE

Litters	2 or 3 a year; period unknown
Young	2–12; naked and helpless
Maturity	from 6 weeks
Longevity	up to *c*2 years

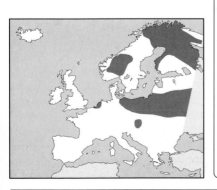

Field Vole *Microtus agrestis*

fairly long fur

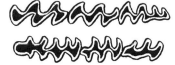

upper molars

lower molars

FIELD VOLE

Type	vole
Habitat	grassland, moorland, arable land
Status	common; locally a pest

PHYSICAL DETAILS

Head & Body	9–14cm
Tail	2.8–5.2cm
Weight	16–60g
Teeth	$\frac{1.0.0.3}{1.0.0.3}$
Colour	dark grey

FOOD AND HABITS

Food	mostly grass and other vegetation
Nest	ball of grasses, often above ground but also in burrow, under logs
Behaviour	nocturnal and diurnal
Voice	squeaks; ultrasonic
Hibernation	none
Migration	none; population cyclic

LIFE CYCLE

Litters	up to 6 a year; spring–autumn
Young	4–6; naked and helpless
Maturity	from 3 weeks
Longevity	less than 2 years

One of the most abundant and widespread voles in Europe. Compared to related voles, it has long, shaggy fur and is slightly darker; the tail is darker above than below. The Field Vole is found in a wide variety of habitats, but particularly in grassland. Runs among the roots of grass are often easily seen. Populations are cyclic, and at their peak attract large numbers of predators such as foxes and owls.

Range: extends from northern Iberia, west to Russia, and north to Britain and Scandinavia; absent from Ireland and most of the Mediterranean area.

Similar Species: very similar to other *Microtus* voles, and can often only be distinguished with certainty by examining the teeth. It is most likely to be confused with the Common Vole (*M. arvalis*), which has shorter fur and paler soles and shorter hind feet.

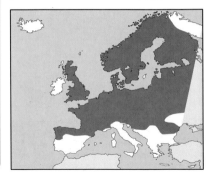

ears concealed

paler than
M. agrestis

upper molars

lower molars

Although it is usually found in grassland, the Common Vole occurs in almost all habitats except dense, coniferous forest. It lives in colonies, with extensive runs and burrows. *Range:* found over most of Europe, except Britain, Ireland and the areas bordering the Mediterranean and most of Scandinavia; however, it is found in the Channel Islands and Orkneys, and also Spitzbergen.
Similar Species: M. epiroticus (=subarvalis) is a distinct species with chromosome differences, but is not distinguishable in the field; it occurs in eastern Europe. *M. gerbei* and *M. rossiae meridionalis* are also very similar. The Common Vole is likely to be confused with other *Microtus* voles. The Field Vole (*M. agrestis*) has longer fur and dark soles, and larger hind feet.

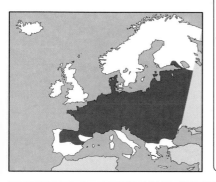

COMMON VOLE

Type	vole
Habitat	grassland
Status	common and widespread

PHYSICAL DETAILS

Head & Body	8–13cm
Tail	2–5cm
Weight	15–50g
Teeth	$\frac{1.0.0.3}{1.0.0.3}$
Colour	grey

FOOD AND HABITS

Food	grasses, other vegetation
Nest	ball of grasses, usually underground, up to 20cm deep
Behaviour	mostly nocturnal, but also diurnal
Voice	squeaks, but mostly silent
Hibernation	none
Migration	none; populations cyclic

LIFE CYCLE

Litters	up to 6 a year; spring–autumn
Young	2–12; naked and helpless
Maturity	from about 3 weeks
Longevity	usually less than 2 years

Balkan Snow Vole *Dinaromys bogdanovi*

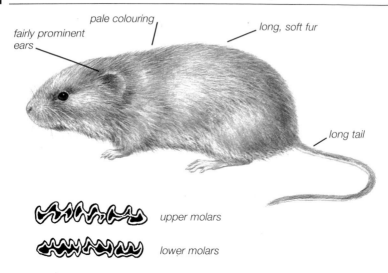

fairly prominent ears

pale colouring

long, soft fur

long tail

upper molars

lower molars

BALKAN SNOW VOLE
Type	vole
Habitat	above tree-line
Status	little known

PHYSICAL DETAILS
Head & Body	10–15.2cm
Tail	6–11cm
Weight	50–80g
Teeth	1.0.0.3
	1.0.0.3
Colour	light grey

FOOD AND HABITS
Food	roots, grasses, other vegetation
Nest	among boulders
Behaviour	nocturnal and diurnal
Voice	unknown
Hibernation	none
Migration	none

LIFE CYCLE
Litters	1 a year; summer
Young	2–3; naked and helpless
Maturity	no data
Longevity	no data

A little-known species of vole, first described in 1922. It has a tail that is relatively long for a vole, and characteristic light grey, long, soft fur and comparatively large ears. The hind feet are also large (usually over 2.2cm long). This species apparently has a low reproductive rate. Recent research suggests that it may comprise two species.

Range: confined to mountain areas of former Yugoslavia, and possibly Albania, but has only rarely been found. It occurs in rocky screes and slopes above the treeline at altitudes of sea level to 2200m.

Similar Species: the Snow Vole (*Chionomys nivalis*), which also has a long tail, is browner, and occurs at lower altitudes.

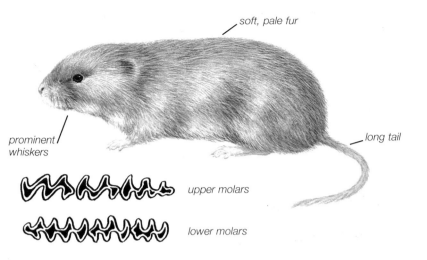

soft, pale fur

prominent whiskers

long tail

upper molars

lower molars

A large vole, with grey fur that becomes increasingly pale with age. The tail is proportionally longer than in most other voles, except the Balkan Snow Vole (*Dinaromys bogdavoni*), the tail of which is normally over 7.5cm. The Snow Vole has a distinctive tooth pattern. It lives in meadows at high altitudes, mostly among rocky screes and talus slopes, up to 4000m in the Alps, but as low as 120m in Montenegro. This vole does not normally tunnel, but makes runs among rocks, on which it can occasionally be seen sunning itself. *Range*: fragmented; it occurs in the larger mountain ranges from Iberia, through southern France, the Alps, and the Appenines, to the mountains of eastern Europe. *Similar Species*: the Balkan Snow Vole – see above; other *Microtus* voles are darker, smaller and have shorter tails.

SNOW VOLE

Type	vole
Habitat	mountain meadows, rocky grassland
Status	numerous isolated populations; not threatened

PHYSICAL DETAILS

Head & Body	8.5–14cm
Tail	4–7.5cm
Weight	35–65g
Teeth	$\underline{1.0.0.3}$
	1.0.0.3
Colour	grey

FOOD AND HABITS

Food	grasses, seeds, berries
Nest	grasses, among rocks
Behaviour	diurnal; colonial
Voice	squeaks, but mostly silent
Hibernation	none
Migration	none

LIFE CYCLE

Litters	up to 2 a year; period unknown
Young	1–5; naked and helpless
Maturity	year following birth
Longevity	less than 2 years

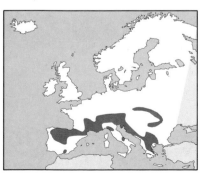

Gunther's Vole *Microtus guentheri*

white paws

very short, pale tail

upper molars

lower molars

GUNTHER'S VOLE

Type	vole
Habitat	grassland
Status	not threatened

PHYSICAL DETAILS

Head & Body	9.7–12.7cm
Tail	2–3.6cm
Weight	33–75g
Teeth	1.0.0.3
	1.0.0.3
Colour	dark grey

FOOD AND HABITS

Food	grasses, roots; sometimes damages crops
Nest	grasses, in burrows
Behaviour	mostly nocturnal
Voice	squeaks, but mostly silent
Hibernation	none
Migration	none

LIFE CYCLE

Litters	2 or more a year; late winter–early spring
Young	6–11, occasionally up to 17; naked and helpless
Maturity	around 1 month
Longevity	no data

This species is very similar to the Common Vole (*M. arvalis*), although for the most part the ranges of the two animals do not overlap. Gunther's Vole has a proportionally shorter tail (less than a quarter of its body length). It is extremely fecund, and population explosions can occur, causing damage to agriculture.

Range: confined to eastern Greece, European Turkey and extreme southern Bulgaria and the Republic of Macedonia.

Similar Species: all other *Microtus* voles, particularly the Common Vole–see above. In Iberia, Cabrera's Vole (*M. cabrerae*) occurs in isolated populations. It is also very similar to the Common Vole and other *Microtus* voles, but has conspicuous long dark hairs on the rump.

ears hardly visible

short tail

upper molars

lower molars

Found in areas with light soil, the Common Pine Vole lives in small colonies and burrows extensively. The colonies can often be detected by the presence of the burrows and spoil heaps of dirt. During inclement weather the vole blocks the entrance to its burrows and retreats underground. It is a largely diurnal species, but is rarely seen owing to its subterranean habits.

Range: It occurs over most of France, eastward to western Russia, and the Baltic republics, and south to northern Italy and northern Greece.

Similar Species: the Alpine Pine Vole, (*M. multiplex*), which can be distinguished with certainty only by differences in the teeth, is confined to the Jura and the southern Alps. The Bavarian Pine Vole (*M. bavaricus*), from the Bavarian Alps, is probably extinct. Other closely related species include M. *dinniki* and M. *tatricus*.

COMMON PINE VOLE	
Type	vole
Habitat	well-vegetated areas
Status	range discontinuous

PHYSICAL DETAILS	
Head & Body	8–10.2cm
Tail	2–4cm
Weight	14–23g
Teeth	1.0.0.3 / 1.0.0.3
Colour	grey

FOOD AND HABITS	
Food	grasses, roots, seeds, etc.
Nest	grasses, in burrows
Behaviour	nocturnal and diurnal
Voice	squeaks, but normally silent
Hibernation	none
Migration	none

LIFE CYCLE	
Litters	2 or 3 a year; spring–summer
Young	2–4; naked and helpless
Maturity	year following birth
Longevity	up to 2 years

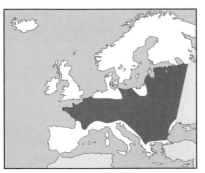

Mediterranean Pine Vole *Microtus duodecimcostatus*

ears hardly visible

yellowish brown

short tail

upper molars

lower molars

MEDITERRANEAN PINE VOLE

Type	vole
Habitat	open woodland
Status	not threatened

PHYSICAL DETAILS

Head & Body	8.5–10.5cm
Tail	2–3cm
Weight	14–23g
Teeth	1.0.0.3
	1.0.0.3
Colour	buff-brown

FOOD AND HABITS

Food	plant matter
Nest	grasses, below ground
Behaviour	nocturnal
Voice	unknown
Hibernation	none
Migration	none

LIFE CYCLE

Litters	probably 1; summer
Young	up to 5; naked and helpless
Maturity	probably 2–3 months
Longevity	probably up to 2 years

This species is superficially very similar in general appearance to other pine voles. The colouring is rather more sandy-buff than in the Common Pine Vole (*M. subterraneus*), but like most other pine voles it can only be distinguished with certainty by tooth characters. Its presence is often indicated by heaps of soil surrounding entrances to burrows.

Range: confined to the southern half of France and most of Iberia, except the north-west.

Similar Species: the closely related Balkan Pine Vole (*M. thomasi*) is very similar but occurs from the Republic of Macedonia to Greece. All pine voles are impossible to identify in the field with any certainty.

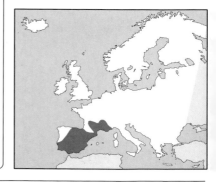

Microtus savii Savi's Pine Vole

short tail

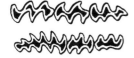

upper molars

lower molars

Like other pine voles this species is almost entirely subterranean and often nocturnal, making it hard to observe. The tunnels may be up to 20cm deep. Although possibly greyer than the Mediterranean Pine Vole (*M. duodecimcostatus*), Savi's can often only be distinguished by tooth characters and detailed measurements.
Range: peninsular Italy, north to the Alps and south-western France.
Similar Species: M. felteni is a little-known species, confined to the central southern Balkans; the Pyrenean Pine Vole (*M. pyrenaicus=gerbei*), is found from the Pyrenees of northern Spain, north to western France; the Lusitanian Pine Vole (*M. lusitanicus*) is confined to the northern half of Iberia and extreme south-western France. These species can be identified only by laboratory examination.

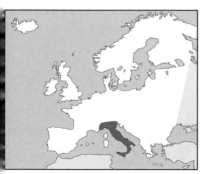

SAVI'S PINE VOLE

Type	vole
Habitat	open woodland
Status	not threatened

PHYSICAL DETAILS

Head & Body	8.2–10.5cm
Tail	2.1–3.5cm
Weight	9–25g
Teeth	1.0.0.3
	1.0.0.3
Colour	buff-brown

FOOD AND HABITS

Food	vegetable matter
Nest	grasses, below ground
Behaviour	largely nocturnal
Voice	unknown
Hibernation	none
Migration	none

LIFE CYCLE

Litters	no data
Young	2–4; naked and helpless
Maturity	probably 2–3 months
Longevity	probably less than 2 years

Northern Water Vole *Arvicola terrestris (=amphibius)*

dark, often blackish

relatively long tail

	NORTHERN WATER VOLE
Type	vole
Habitat	wetlands, meadows and fields
Status	possibly declining in UK; not known to be threatened elsewhere

PHYSICAL DETAILS

Head & Body	12–20cm
Tail	8–13cm
Weight	60–200g
Teeth	1.0.0.3 1.0.0.3
Colour	pale brown to blackish

FOOD AND HABITS

Food	mostly vegetable matter; also fish and carrion
Nest	grasses, underground
Behaviour	diurnal and nocturnal; often easily visible
Voice	squeaks and chatters
Hibernation	none
Migration	none

LIFE CYCLE

Litters	3–4 a year; period unknown
Young	4–6; naked and helpless
Maturity	2 months
Longevity	up to 4 years

This large vole is very variable in colour, ranging from sandy brown to almost black. It is usually found in wetland habitats, but also occurs well away from water. Those living away from water are around half the weight of aquatic forms. When tunnelling, in meadows and pastures, it often throws up tumps of soil. These are similar to molehills, although the soil is finer. The entrance to a water vole's tunnel is oblique, whereas that of a mole is vertical. Occasionally, moles and water voles share the same tunnels.

Range: most of Europe except north-western France, Iberia and the southern Balkans. It occurs on Sicily but is absent from most other Mediterranean islands and from Ireland.

Similar Species: the range of the Southern Water Vole (*A. sapidus*) overlaps in France and northern Spain.

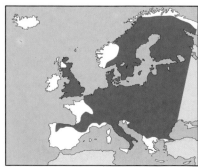

Arvicola sapidus Southern Water Vole

larger and darker
than *A. terrestris*

The Southern Water Vole is extremely similar to the Northern (*A. amphibius*) and was only distinguished in 1963. It differs in being larger and having a longer cheek tooth row (more than 1cm long). In areas where the two species overlap, the Southern is generally found in more aquatic habitats.

Range: this species replaces the Northern Water Vole over much of France and most of Spain. It may occur in the extreme south-west of Belgium and in Luxembourg.

Similar Species: the Northern Water Vole which is smaller – see above. When swimming, water voles are most likely to be confused with the Brown Rat (*Rattus norvegicus*), which swims with most of its body on the surface of the water and has a longer tail.

SOUTHERN WATER VOLE

Type	vole
Habitat	wetlands, grassland
Status	not threatened

PHYSICAL DETAILS

Head & Body	17–22cm
Tail	10.5–13.5cm
Weight	120–280g
Teeth	$\frac{1.0.0.3}{1.0.0.3}$
Colour	dark brown

FOOD AND HABITS

Food	mostly vegetation; also some animal matter, particularly carrion
Nest	grasses, in burrows
Behaviour	nocturnal and diurnal
Voice	probably squeaks and chatters
Hibernation	none
Migration	none

LIFE CYCLE

Litters	3–4 a year; spring–autumn
Young	2–8; blind and helpless
Maturity	2–3 months
Longevity	probably up to 4 years

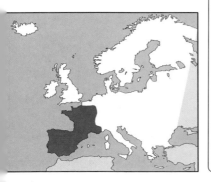

Guinea Pig *Cavia porcellus*

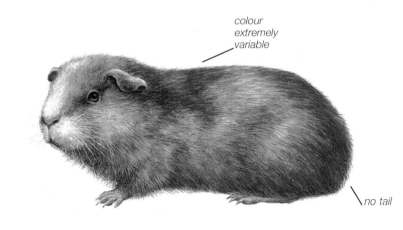

colour
extremely
variable

no tail

	GUINEA PIG
Type	cavy
Habitat	gardens, waste ground
Status	domesticated

	PHYSICAL DETAILS
Head & Body	up to c25cm
Tail	none
Weight	up to 1kg
Teeth	1.0.0.3
	1.0.0.3
Colour	extremely variable

	FOOD AND HABITS
Food	exclusively vegetarian
Nest	none
Behaviour	diurnal
Voice	whistles, squeaks
Hibernation	none
Migration	none

	LIFE CYCLE
Litters	2–3 a year; spring–autumn
Young	1–9, usually 2–3; fully furred and active
Maturity	3–4 weeks
Longevity	3–4 years in wild

The Guinea Pig is a domesticated species originally from the Andes of South America. Its precise ancestry is not clear and the domesticated forms occur in a wide range of colours as well as with long hair (Peruvian) and rosetted fur (Abysinian). They are popular pets and occasionally escape and can survive in the wild and breed, though they do not appear to have become established anywhere in Europe. They are colonial, diurnal and highly vocal, making a wide range of whistles, and squeaks. They can be distinguished from all other similar sized animals by their compact shape and lack of a tail.

Range: occurs sporadically throughout Europe as an escape around human settlements, such as in gardens.

Similar Species: not likely to be confused with any other species.

flattened,
scaly tail

A large aquatic rodent with webbed hind feet and a long tail. Muskrats build lodges from vegetation and twigs, and also use feeding platforms. At least one entrance to the lodge is underwater. The diet comprises aquatic vegetation, and also crops and some animal matter. Muskrats usually live in pairs.
Range: originally from North America, the Muskrat was widely bred in captivity for its fur (musquash), and the descendants of escapes have now spread over much of Europe.
Similar Species: the Beaver (*Castor fiber*) is larger, with a flattened tail; the Brown Rat (*Rattus norvegicus*) and water voles (*Arvicola* species) are smaller. The Coypu (*Myocastor coypus*) is larger. It is another introduction, from South America, occurring mostly in France, but also in Germany and Italy.

MUSKRAT

Type	vole
Habitat	wetlands
Status	introduced; often a pest

PHYSICAL DETAILS

Head & Body	25–40cm
Tail	19–25cm
Weight	600–2400g
Teeth	$\frac{1.0.0.3}{1.0.0.3}$
Colour	dark brown above, paler below

FOOD AND HABITS

Food	mostly vegetation; some animal matter
Nest	large lodge in water
Behaviour	nocturnal and diurnal
Voice	normally silent
Hibernation	none
Migration	none

LIFE CYCLE

Litters	1–4 a year; period unknown
Young	5–10; blind and nearly naked
Maturity	year following birth
Longevity	up to 7–8 years

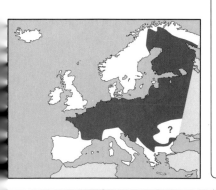

Balkan Mole Rat *Spalax graecus*

eyes invisible

prominent incisors

no tail

GREATER MOLE RAT

Type	mole rat
Habitat	open grasslands, farmland
Status	not threatened

PHYSICAL DETAILS

Head & Body	15–27cm
Tail	none
Weight	140–220g
Teeth	1.0.0.3
	1.0.0.3
Colour	yellow-brown above, darker below

FOOD AND HABITS

Food	roots and tubers; often stored in burrows
Nest	under mound of soil excavated from burrows
Behaviour	nocturnal and diurnal; lives underground
Voice	unknown
Hibernation	none
Migration	none

LIFE CYCLE

Litters	3–4 a year; spring–autumn
Young	usually 2–4, up to 9; naked and helpless
Maturity	no data
Longevity	no data

A thickset, blunt-headed rodent with no tail and non-functional eyes concealed in fur. It digs with its teeth and at the centre of its tunnel system has a large mound, with a nest beneath. It is found in open steppes, grasslands, and farmland where it feeds on roots and tubers, sometimes causing damage to agriculture. It only occasionally comes above ground, to bask in the sun. *Range:* fragmented distribution in the Republic of Macedonia and Greece, north to the south-western Ukraine. *Similar Species:* the identification of mole rats is difficult and there is still much confusion over the identity of many populations. The Lesser Mole Rat (*Nannospulax leucodon*) is found from Croatia east to the Ukraine.

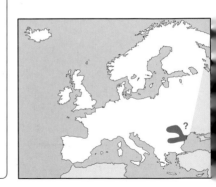

'greasy' appearance

long, scaly tail

A serious and widespread pest, the Brown Rat is one of the best-known mammals in Europe. The fur colour is variable but is usually dark brown with a greasy appearance. As well as destroying stored food, this rat also causes extensive damage to property, and carries many diseases transmissable to man and other animals. It is extremely fecund and adaptable, preferring damp habitats, including sewers.

Range: occurs throughout most of northern and central Europe, but is less widespread in the Mediterranean area, where it is replaced by the Black Rat (*R. rattus*).

Similar Species: most likely to be confused with the Black Rat, particularly in the south of its range. The Black Rat is more mouse-like, with a longer tail, and larger ears.

BROWN RAT	
Type	rat
Habitat	ubiquitous
Status	abundant pest

PHYSICAL DETAILS	
Head & Body	20–28cm
Tail	17–23cm
Weight	270–580g
Teeth	1.0.0.3
	1.0.0.3
Colour	brown

FOOD AND HABITS	
Food	omnivorous
Nest	grass, paper or similar material, in hole or burrow
Behaviour	sociable; mostly nocturnal
Voice	variety of squeaks
Hibernation	none
Migration	none

LIFE CYCLE	
Litters	up to 5 a year; at any time of year
Young	up to 15, usually 7–8; naked and helpless
Maturity	3–4 months
Longevity	2–3 years in wild; longer as a pet

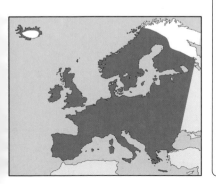

Black Rat *Rattus rattus*

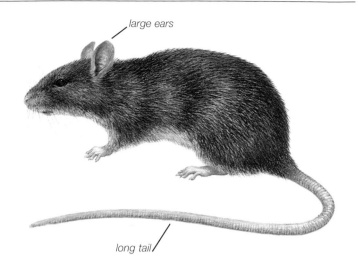

large ears

long tail

BLACK RAT	
Type	rat
Habitat	ubiquitous
Status	pest

PHYSICAL DETAILS	
Head & Body	16–24cm
Tail	18–26cm
Weight	135–250g
Teeth	1.0.0.3
	1.0.0.3
Colour	brownish or blackish

FOOD AND HABITS	
Food	omnivorous, but prefers fruit
Nest	grasses, paper, refuse, rags, in cavity, tree or bush
Behaviour	mostly nocturnal
Voice	wide range of squeaks
Hibernation	none
Migration	none

LIFE CYCLE	
Litters	up to 5 a year; at any time of year
Young	usually 7–8, up to 16; naked and helpless
Maturity	3 months
Longevity	2–3 years in wild

A familiar rodent in many parts of Europe, the Black Rat is an adaptable species, living in a wide range of habitats. In contrast to the Brown Rat (*R. norvegicus*), it prefers locations above ground level, frequently living in attics and even in trees. Its fur colour is variable, ranging from almost black to sandy brown. It is omnivorous, feeding on crops, stored foodstuffs, and refuse. *Range:* widespread and abundant in Mediterranean Europe, but becoming increasingly fragmented in northern Europe, and now on the brink of extinction in Scandinavia and Britain. Scattered, isolated populations occur in the Czech Republic, Slovakia and the Baltic Republics.
Similar Species: the Brown Rat is larger and its fur has a greasy sheen.

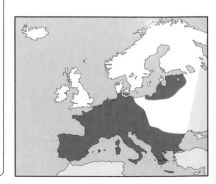

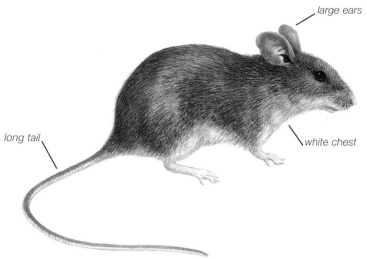

large ears

long tail

white chest

A small, large-eyed and large-eared mouse with a long slender tail. It is sandy brown above and white below. The Wood Mouse is very agile, and often climbs. It occurs in a wide variety of wooded habitats, and often enters houses. Although mostly vegetarian, often using an old bird's nest as a feeding platform, it also eats grubs and other invertebrates. *Range:* one of the most widespread small mammals in Europe, occurring over almost the entire continent except the north-eastern regions; it also occurs on most islands.
Similar Species: the Pygmy Field Mice (*A. microps* and *A. uralensis*) are like a small Wood Mouse, with a body length of less than 9.6cm. They are found in eastern Europe. The Wood Mouse lacks the broad chest-band of the Yellow-necked Mouse (*A. flavicolis*), and is yellower than most other mice.

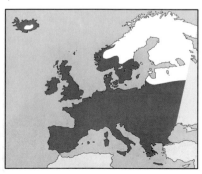

WOOD MOUSE

Type	mouse
Habitat	mostly wooded habitats, but also more open areas
Status	not threatened

PHYSICAL DETAILS

Head & Body	7.5–11cm
Tail	7–11cm
Weight	15–32g
Teeth	$\frac{1.0.0.3}{1.0.0.3}$
Colour	sandy brown above, white below

FOOD AND HABITS

Food	mostly seeds, berries, bark and other vegetable material; also some animal matter
Nest	grasses, in cavity, old bird's nest, under log
Behaviour	mostly nocturnal
Voice	mostly silent; some squeaks and chirps
Hibernation	none
Migration	none

LIFE CYCLE

Litters	up to 4 a year; spring–autumn
Young	3–9; naked and helpless
Maturity	2 months
Longevity	1–2 years

Yellow-necked Mouse *Apodemus flavicollis*

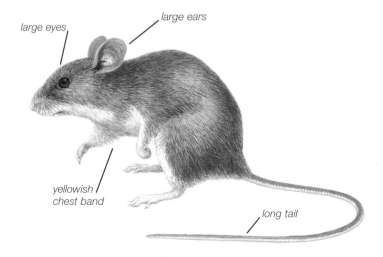

large eyes

large ears

yellowish chest band

long tail

YELLOW-NECKED MOUSE

Type	mouse
Habitat	mostly woodland; also orchards, gardens, hedgerows
Status	not threatened

PHYSICAL DETAILS

Head & Body	8–13cm
Tail	8.7–13cm
Weight	18–50g
Teeth	1.0.0.3 1.0.0.3
Colour	yellowish brown above, white below, with yellowish chest band

FOOD AND HABITS

Food	seeds, berries, fruit, other vegetable matter; also insects
Nest	grasses and leaves in cavity; often in bird or bat boxes
Behaviour	mostly nocturnal
Voice	squeaks and chatters but mostly silent
Hibernation	none
Migration	none

LIFE CYCLE

Litters	up to 3 a year; spring–summer
Young	2–9; naked and helpless
Maturity	2–3 months
Longevity	1–2 years

Very similar to the closely related Wood Mouse (*A. sylvaticus*), but generally found in more thickly wooded habitats. It often enters houses and outbuildings in autumn and winter. The eyes and ears are large and the yellowish colouring of the upperparts extends across the chest in a characteristic band.
Range: widespread in central Europe and more scattered in the west, extending as far as southern England and northern Spain. It also occurs south to Italy and Greece.
Similar Species: most likely to be confused with other *Apodemus* species, most of which are smaller. The Rock Mouse (*A. mystacinus*) is larger, greyer, and occurs in more open, scrubby areas. *A. alpicola* occurs in the Alps.

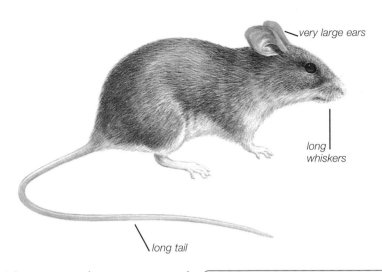

very large ears

long whiskers

long tail

A large mouse with prominent eyes and ears, and a long tail. It is slightly larger and greyer than the Yellow-necked Mouse (*A. flavicollis*), and always lacks a throat patch. Its scientific name comes from its prominent whiskers – the longest are over 4.7cm, whereas those of the Yellow-necked Mouse and other *Apodemus* mice are under 4cm. Found mostly in rocky open habitats up to 1620m, the Rock Mouse lives among crevices, but rarely burrows. It feeds mostly on seeds and other vegetable matter. This species is sometimes known as the Broad-toothed Field Mouse.
Range: extends from the Adriatic coast of Slovenia to Greece and Crete.
Similar Species: all other *Apodemus* mice are smaller and generally more yellow-brown. It could be confused with the Black Rat (*Rattus rattus*), which is larger and more robust.

ROCK MOUSE
Type mouse
Habitat rocky hillsides
Status not threatened

PHYSICAL DETAILS
Head & Body 8.5–15cm
Tail 10–14.4cm
Weight 28–64g
Teeth $\frac{1.0.0.3}{1.0.0.3}$
Colour greyish above; white below

FOOD AND HABITS
Food seeds and other vegetable matter
Nest none known
Behaviour mostly nocturnal
Voice unknown
Hibernation none
Migration none

LIFE CYCLE
Litters 1–3 a year; spring–autumn
Young 4–6; naked and helpless
Maturity probably less than 3 months
Longevity probably 1–2 years

Striped Field Mouse *Apodemus agrarius*

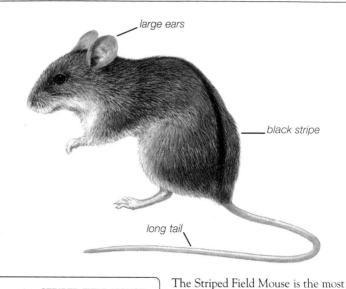

large ears

black stripe

long tail

	STRIPED FIELD MOUSE
Type	mouse
Habitat	dense vegetation, often near water
Status	not threatened, but several isolated populations

PHYSICAL DETAILS

Head & Body	7–12.5cm
Tail	6.5–9cm
Weight	12–39g
Teeth	1.0.0.3 / 1.0.0.3
Colour	sandy brown above with dark median stripe; greyish below

FOOD AND HABITS

Food	mostly seeds; also insects
Nest	none
Behaviour	mostly nocturnal
Voice	unknown
Hibernation	none
Migration	none

LIFE CYCLE

Litters	2–3 a year; spring–summer
Young	4–9; naked and helpless
Maturity	probably less than 3 months
Longevity	up to 4 years

The Striped Field Mouse is the most distinctive of the *Apodemus* mice. It is about the same size as a Wood Mouse (*A. sylvaticus*), but has a characteristic dark stripe down the centre of the back. The tail is shorter than the head and body. This species occurs in dense vegetation, often along rivers, and feeds mainly on seeds, but also on insects and their grubs. It lives in burrows, and in winter often invades houses.

Range: widespread in Russia, the Ukraine and eastern Europe but more fragmented further westward; isolated populations are found in Finland, western Germany, Denmark and northern Italy. It occurs as far south as northern Greece and European Turkey.

Similar Species: the only other species with a dark stripe are the birch mice, which have long, slender tails.

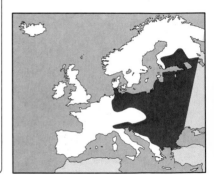

yellowish or reddish brown

grass net woven among grasses or crops

prehensile tail

white

With a body length that barely reaches 8cm the Harvest Mouse is one of the smallest European mammals. In winter and early summer it spends much of its time in burrows. In late summer it builds globular grass nests among the stems of plants such as grasses, reeds and cereal crops. When climbing it uses its prehensile tail for support. This mouse is best easily found by searching for its nests in early autumn, as the dying vegetation makes the nests more obvious.

Range: occurs over much of Europe from northern Spain, north to southern Britain and Denmark, east to Finland and Russia and south to northern Italy and Bulgaria and European Turkey, but is absent from most of Greece and former Yugoslavia.

Similar Species: not likely to be confused with any other species.

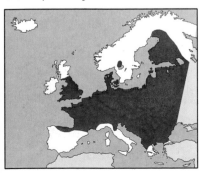

HARVEST MOUSE

Type	mouse
Habitat	meadows, reed beds, ditches, agricultural lands
Status	not threatened

PHYSICAL DETAILS

Head & Body	5–7.8cm
Tail	4–7.5cm
Weight	3.5–13g
Teeth	$\frac{1.0.0.3}{1.0.0.3}$
Colour	orange-brown above; white below

FOOD AND HABITS

Food	mostly seeds and insects
Nest	none
Behaviour	diurnal and nocturnal
Voice	mostly silent
Hibernation	none
Migration	none

LIFE CYCLE

Litters	usually 3, up to 7, a year; spring–autumn
Young	3–7; naked and helpless
Maturity	6 weeks
Longevity	up to 3 years, usually less

Western House Mouse *Mus domesticus*

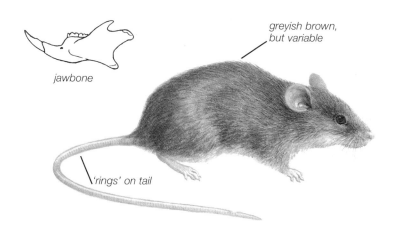

greyish brown, but variable

jawbone

'rings' on tail

WESTERN HOUSE MOUSE

Type	mouse
Habitat	usually associated with human habitations
Status	not threatened; often pest

PHYSICAL DETAILS

Head & Body	7.5–9.5cm
Tail	7–9.5cm
Weight	up to 25g
Teeth	$\frac{1.0.0.3}{1.0.0.3}$
Colour	grey-brown above, darker below

FOOD AND HABITS

Food	omnivorous; particularly seeds and grain
Nest	leaves, paper; untidy
Voice	squeaks
Behaviour	nocturnal and diurnal
Hibernation	none
Migration	none

LIFE CYCLE

Litters	5–10 a year; throughout the year
Young	usually up to 9; naked and helpless
Maturity	6 weeks
Longevity	usually less than 2 years

It has recently been shown that there is more than one species of house mouse in Europe. They cannot, however, be distinguished with certainty in the field. The Western species is brownish grey above, paler below. It occurs in a wide range of habitats, mostly close to human habitations, where it often causes damage to stored foodstuffs.
Range: west of Denmark and the Adriatic.
Similar Species: the Eastern House Mouse (*M. musculus*), which is slightly larger, with a paler belly. It occurs in Sweden, eastern Denmark and Europe east of the Adriatic and the river Elbe, and commonly lives in human habitations. The Alpine House Mouse (*M. poschiavinus*), from southern Switzerland and the Italian Alps, is distinguishable from other house mice only by its chromosomes.

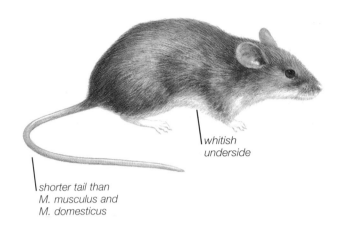

whitish underside

shorter tail than M. musculus and M. domesticus

The Algerian House Mouse is similar to other house mice, but is smaller, has whitish underparts and is often browner above. Like other house mice it is often associated with human habitations, but also often occurs in scrub, woodland, and agricultural land. It appears to be less gregarious than other species.
Range: confined to Iberia and Mediterranean France.
Similar Species: other house mice – see above. The Steppe Mouse (*M. hortulanus*), which occurs in steppe habitats of south-eastern Europe, has similar sharply contrasting upper and lower colouration. The Mediterranean House Mouse (*M. abbotti*) occurs in the Republic of Macedonia and Greece eastwards to Asia Minor, and is distinguishable from the Steppe Mouse by minor tooth characters.

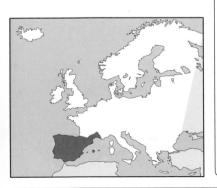

ALGERIAN HOUSE MOUSE

Type	mouse
Habitat	gardens, open woodland, scrub
Status	not threatened; often pest

PHYSICAL DETAILS

Head & Body	6.7–8.8cm
Tail	5.2–7.4cm
Weight	10–15g
Teeth	1.0.0.3 / 1.0.0.3
Colour	grey-brown above; grey-white below

FOOD AND HABITS

Food	omnivorous; particularly seeds and grain
Nest	grasses and leaves in cavity or burrow
Behaviour	nocturnal and diurnal
Voice	squeaks
Hibernation	none
Migration	none

LIFE CYCLE

Litters	5–10 a year; throughout the year
Young	usually up to 9
Maturity	6 weeks
Longevity	usually less than 2 years

Cretan Spiny Mouse *Acomys cahirinus*

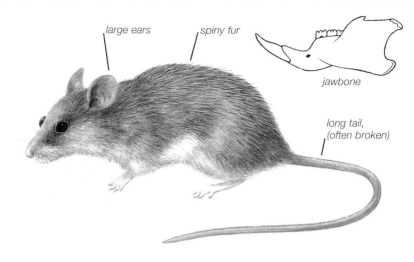

large ears

spiny fur

jawbone

long tail,
(often broken)

	SPINY MOUSE
Type	mouse
Habitat	dry scrub, gardens, agricultural land, hillsides
Status	not threatened

	PHYSICAL DETAILS
Head & Body	9–12.5cm
Tail	8–12cm (often broken)
Weight	30–86g
Teeth	$\frac{1.0.0.3}{1.0.0.3}$
Colour	yellowish brown above; whitish below

	FOOD AND HABITS
Food	mostly seeds; also snails and insects
Nest	none, or rudimentary
Behaviour	nocturnal and diurnal
Voice	unknown
Hibernation	none
Migration	none

	LIFE CYCLE
Litters	several; at almost any time of year
Young	1–5 (usually 2 or 3); naked and helpless
Maturity	about 1 month
Longevity	usually 2–3 years, up to 5 years

Similiar in size and colouring to *Apodemus* mice, this species is easily recognized at close quarters by the stiff, spiny hairs on its back. It is found mostly in dry scrubby habitats, including olive groves and rocky hillsides, and often enters human habitations. If handled or attacked by a predator, the tail breaks easily, and animals with only stumps are common. *Range:* confined to Crete. A closely related species is widespread in Africa and Asia.
Similar Species: most likely to be confused with the Wood Mouse (*Apodemus sylvaticus*), and the Eastern House Mouse (*Mus musculus*), neither of which have spiny fur.

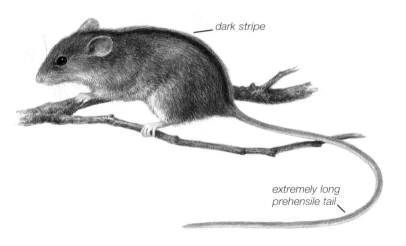

Sicista betulina # Northern Birch Mouse

dark stripe

extremely long
prehensile tail

A small, rather slender mouse with an exceptionally long tail and a distinctive dark stripe down the middle of the back. It is found in forests and more open areas, generally in damp places such as bogs and mountain meadows with dense vegetation; it is often associated with birch, particularly in the north. This species is an agile climber, using its prehensile tail for support. From late summer to spring it hibernates.
Range: the centre of its European distribution is in western Russia and southern Finland; elsewhere the range is rather fragmented, and associated with mountainous habitats in the south.
Similar Species: the Southern Birch Mouse (*S. subtilis*), which has a proportionally shorter tail, greyer upperparts, and a dark stripe, that is thinner, has a pale border and occurs only on the lower half of the back.

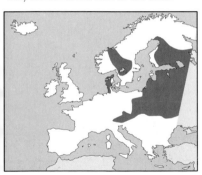

NORTHERN BIRCH MOUSE

Type	mouse
Habitat	dense vegetation in forests and meadows
Status	not threatened, but fragmented in south and west

PHYSICAL DETAILS

Head & Body	5–7.8cm
Tail	7–10.5cm
Weight	5–13g
Teeth	$\frac{1.0.1.3}{1.0.0.3}$
Colour	brown above, with dark median stripe; paler below

FOOD AND HABITS

Food	seeds, berries; also insects
Nest	globular; made of grasses, in hole, tussock or crevice
Behaviour	nocturnal and diurnal
Voice	unknown
Hibernation	late summer–spring; in underground nest
Migration	none

LIFE CYCLE

Litters	1 a year; late spring–early summer
Young	2–11; naked and helpless
Maturity	11 months
Longevity	3–4 years

Southern Birch Mouse *Sicista subtilis*

dark stripe
bordered with
pale stripe

extremely long
prehensile tail

SOUTHERN BIRCH MOUSE

Type	mouse
Habitat	open woodland, grassland and scrub
Status	some isolated western populations may be threatened

PHYSICAL DETAILS

Head & Body	5–7.2cm
Tail	6.7–8.5cm
Weight	8–14g
Teeth	1.0.1.3 1.0.0.3
Colour	brown above, light brown below, with pale-bordered median stripe

FOOD AND HABITS

Food	insects and seeds
Nest	none
Behaviour	mostly nocturnal
Voice	unknown
Hibernation	autumn–spring; underground
Migration	none

LIFE CYCLE

Litters	1 a year; summer
Young	2–7; naked and helpless
Maturity	probably 3–4 years
Longevity	up to 3 years

A close relation of the Northern Birch Mouse (*S. betulina*), to which it is very similar. The tail is long and prehensile, but shorter than the Northern's. The dark stripe on the back often stops short of the head, and is bordered with a pale stripe either side. It occurs in rather more open habitats than the Northern species, and the hibernation period is shorter.

Range: rather fragmented distribution, extending from Austria, Czech Republic and Hungary eastwards through Romania and the extreme north-east of Bulgaria and the Ukraine, and north to southern Poland.

Similar Species: the Northern Birch Mouse—see above. The one other mouse with a dorsal stripe is the Striped Field Mouse (*Apodemus agrarius*), which has a shorter, non-prehensile tail.

no tail

♂

The Barbary Macaque is the only primate found living in the wild in Europe, although it was actually introduced to Gibraltar from North Africa. It is tame and lives in troops of up to 30. This is the only monkey to completely lack a tail.

Range: confined to Gibraltar, where the population has been maintained by occasional introductions from its native North Africa. In its native habitats the Barbary Macaque is endangered, largely through severe habitat disturbance, particularly intensive logging. The Gibraltar population is culled regularly to prevent an excessive build-up of numbers.

Similar Species: none.

BARBARY MACAQUE

Type	monkey
Habitat	rocky hillsides
Status	endangered in North Africa

PHYSICAL DETAILS

Head & Body	60–70cm
Tail	absent
Weight	5–15kg
Teeth	2.1.2.3
	2.1.2.3
Colour	greyish brown above, with darker face; paler below

FOOD AND HABITS

Food	omnivorous, but those in Gibraltar are fed by humans
Nest	none
Behaviour	diurnal
Voice	chattering
Hibernation	none
Migration	none

LIFE CYCLE

Litters	1 every other year; at any time of year
Young	usually 1; furred, but dependent on mother
Maturity	3–4 years
Longevity	up to 15 years

Polar Bear *Ursus maritimus*

white or yellowish

POLAR BEAR

Type	bear
Habitat	polar ice caps and tundra
Status	out of danger

PHYSICAL DETAILS

Head & Body	1.6–2.5m
Tail	8–10cm
Weight	400–450kg, occasionally 750kg
Teeth	$\frac{3.1.2.2}{3.1.2.2}$
Colour	white or yellowish

FOOD AND HABITS

Food	seals, fish, sea birds and carrion
Nest	excavates den in snow in winter
Behaviour	diurnal
Voice	normally silent; roars and grunts occasionally
Hibernation	autumn–early spring; in den
Migration	moves north in summer; wanders widely

LIFE CYCLE

Litters	1 every other year; autumn–early spring
Young	usually 1, occasionally 2; naked and helpless
Maturity	in 2nd summer
Longevity	up to 33 years in captivity, less in wild

An unmistakable, huge, white or yellowish bear. Usually found only in the extreme north, Polar Bears are most often seen close to the sea, on ice or actually swimming. They only rarely occur further south, drifting with an iceberg. Mostly carnivorous, they feed on seals, fish and birds, although in summer they may eat berries as well as lichens and mosses. The females spend the winter in a den excavated in snow, giving birth to one or two tiny cubs (about 500g) after a gestation of about 240 days. The cubs first leave the den when they are about 4 months old. Although once seriously threatened by overhunting, Polar Bears have now rebuilt their numbers in most parts of their range and are no longer considered endangered.
Range: confined to polar regions.
Similar Species: none.

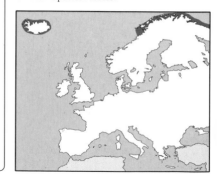

right
fore

left
hind

The Brown Bear is one of the largest carnivores, although European bears are much smaller than those of North America. They are normally very shy but can be aggressive in defence of their cubs. An omnivorous diet includes grasses and shoots in spring, as well as grubs, birds' eggs, rodents and honey. In autumn they feed on berries and fruits, and accumulate a thick layer of fat before hibernation. Brown Bears are usually solitary, but the female is often accompanied by her cubs until they reach independence.

Range: once found over almost all of Europe, including Britain, but now extinct in western Europe except for a few isolated populations in Spain, the the Pyrenees and Italy. They are still reasonably widespread in Scandinavia and eastern Europe.

Similar Species: none

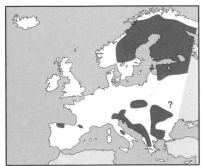

BROWN BEAR

Type	bear
Habitat	forest, woodland, often in mountains
Status	endangered; protected

PHYSICAL DETAILS

Head & Body	up to 2m
Tail	vestigial
Weight	usually 150–250kg, up to 480kg
Teeth	3.1.4.2 3.1.4.3
Colour	dark brown

FOOD AND HABITS

Food	omnivorous
Nest	den among roots in cave or hollow tree
Behaviour	diurnal and nocturnal
Voice	growls
Hibernation	rather light; easily woken autumn–spring; in den
Migration	moves to high mountains in summer

LIFE CYCLE

Litters	1 every other year; winter–early spring
Young	1–2; tiny, naked and helpless
Maturity	in 3rd year
Longevity	30–40 years

Wolf *Canis lupus*

tail down

right fore

left hind

WOLF

Type	dog
Habitat	once ubiquitous, now confined to remote mountains and northern tundra
Status	extinct or endangered in Europe

PHYSICAL DETAILS

Head & Body	1–1.6m
Tail	35–50cm
Weight	30–80kg
Teeth	3.1.4.2
	3.1.4.3
Colour	whitish, grey or yellowish with black or reddish colouring on back

FOOD AND HABITS

Food	carnivorous, preying mostly on mammals; occasionally eats fruit
Nest	den among rocks, tree roots
Behaviour	mostly nocturnal
Voice	howls, yaps
Hibernation	none
Migration	wanders extensively and follows migrations of reindeer

LIFE CYCLE

Litters	1; late winter–spring
Young	3–10; blind and helpless
Maturity	2 years
Longevity	up to 16 years

The Wolf is the ancestor of the Domestic Dog, with which it freely interbreeds. Wolves normally live in packs led by a dominant female. Their appearance varies geographically, with those from the north being larger with thicker fur. They feed principally on mammals such as deer, but also predate domestic livestock. After centuries of persecution, Wolves are very shy and usually nocturnal.

Range: once widespread throughout Europe, including the British Isles, the Wolf is now extinct or on the brink of extinction and seriously endangered. Isolated populations occur in Spain, Portugal, Italy and Scandinavia, and also in eastern Europe.

Similar Species: Domestic and Feral Dogs *(C. familiaris)* have larger ears and a more upright tail. The Jackal *(C. aureus)* is smaller.

variety of types

ears often flopped

tail normally upright

colours variable, often piebald

right fore

Feral Dogs are extremely variable in appearance, showing the characteristics of a wide variety of domestic dogs, with which they frequently interbreed. They do, however, have a tendency to revert to a vaguely Jackal-like form, though often with patches of white or black. Small packs scavenge near human habitations, even in cities. In all aspects of their breeding biology they are identical with domestic dogs.
Range: widespread and often surprisingly numerous in many parts of Europe, particularly in the south.
Similar Species: in the south of its range the Feral Dog is most likely to be confused with the Jackal (*C. aureus*), but the latter always has a bobbed tail, and does not have white or black patches on its coat.

FERAL DOG

Type	dog
Habitat	usually close to human habitations
Status	generally considered a pest

PHYSICAL DETAILS

Head & Body	variable: up to 1.5m
Tail	very variable; up to 50cm
Weight	variable; up to 50kg
Teeth	3.1.4.2
	3.1.4.3
Colour	very variable; often similar to domestic dogs

FOOD AND HABITS

Food	mostly carrion and garbage
Nest	den under derelict buildings or in burrows
Behaviour	diurnal and nocturnal
Voice	barks; also howls
Hibernation	none
Migration	none

LIFE CYCLE

Litters	1 or 2 a year; at any time of year
Young	up to 10, usually 4–8; blind and helpless
Maturity	6–8 months
Longevity	usually 4–5 years

Jackal *Canis aureus*

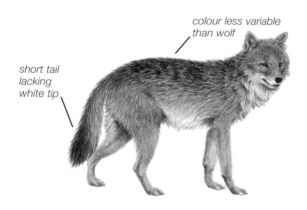

colour less variable than wolf

short tail lacking white tip

JACKAL
Type dog
Habitat generally around towns and villages
Status endangered in Europe

PHYSICAL DETAILS
Head & Body 71–85cm
Tail 20–30cm
Weight 7–15kg
Teeth 3.1.4.2
3.1.4.3
Colour greyish, tinged black on back

FOOD AND HABITS
Food mostly carrion; also insects and other small animals, and fruit
Nest dens among rocks in thickets, burrows
Behaviour mostly nocturnal; diurnal away from humans
Voice howl, followed by barks
Hibernation none
Migration none

LIFE CYCLE
Litters 1 a year; in spring
Young 3–9; blind and helpless
Maturity 2nd year
Longevity up to 14 years, but normally less

The Jackal is midway between the Red Fox *(Vulpes vulpes)* and the Wolf (C. *lupus)* in size and has markings rather like a German Shepherd Dog, though it is smaller with a bob tail. Jackals usually occur in pairs or small family groups. In Europe they are found mostly around the outskirts of villages and rural towns, where they scavenge rubbish tips, often in association with Feral Dogs (C. *familiaris).* They also feed on carrion, and raid poultry and crops. Scavengers may be seen along beaches of rivers and coasts.
Range: confined to south-eastern Europe as far north as Romania and Hungary. Little is known of its current status in Europe, and it may be declining or extinct in many areas.
Similar Species: Wolf and Red Fox. The Feral Dog usually lacks a bob tail and may have black or white patches.

prominent ears

left fore

right hind

bushy tail

white tip

droppings

The Red Fox is generally a bright rufous red, with a white-tipped tail. The backs of the ears and the paws and lower limbs are blackish. Dark grey, blackish and brown forms also occur. Foxes are found in a wide variety of habitats, including cities and villages, where they raid garbage. Although they kill livestock, they feed mostly on small mammals, as well as insects, fruit and berries. The trails are direct. Foxes are agile and cat-like; in spotlights the eye-shine is similar to a cat's.

Range: has the widest distribution of any European mammal, occurring from the Arctic to the Mediterranean, and on many islands, but not Crete or Iceland.

Similar Species: in the north of its range it may be confused with the Arctic Fox (*Alopex lagopus*), which lacks the white tail tip, and in the south-east, the Jackal (*Canis aureus*), which is more dog-like.

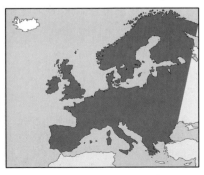

RED FOX

Type	dog
Habitat	ubiquitous
Status	common in most of range; hunted for pelts and 'sport'

PHYSICAL DETAILS

Head & Body	60–90cm
Tail	40–60cm
Weight	5–10kg
Teeth	3.1.4.2
	3.1.4.3
Colour	reddish above; white below and on tail tip; ears and paws often blackish

FOOD AND HABITS

Food	mostly small animals; also fruit and poultry
Nest	den in burrow
Behaviour	mostly nocturnal
Voice	yips and a scream in breeding season
Hibernation	none
Migration	may move down from high altitudes during winter; otherwise none

LIFE CYCLE

Litters	1; early spring
Young	usually 4–6, occasionally more; blind and helpless
Maturity	9–11 months
Longevity	10 years or more in captivity, less in wild

Arctic Fox *Alopex lagopus*

blue form

summer

winter

ARCTIC FOX
Type dog
Habitat tundra and boreal forest
Status common in most of range

PHYSICAL DETAILS
Head & Body 50–85cm
Tail 25–55cm
Weight 3–8kg
Teeth 3.1.4.2
3.1.4.3
Colour white, brownish or bluish grey

FOOD AND HABITS
Food small mammals, particularly lemmings; also carrion, fruit
Nest extensive burrows, often used for many years
Behaviour nocturnal and diurnal
Voice a variety of barks
Hibernation none
Migration wanders extensively

LIFE CYCLE
Litters usually 1 a year; spring–summer
Young usually 7–10, up to 21; blind and helpless
Maturity 9–10 months
Longevity 8–10 years

Although pure white in winter, and brownish grey above and yellowish white below in summer, this fox also occurs in a 'blue' phase, which is bluish grey in winter, and darker in summer. The Arctic Fox has made some of the longest movements ever recorded for a terrestrial mammal. The dens are colonial and often extensive. They may be used for several centuries, and the vegetation that grows on the soil enriched by the droppings often differs from the surrounding countryside. Arctic Fox numbers fluctuate widely from year to year.
Range: widespread and often abundant in the Arctic, usually above the tree-line. It is also found on many Arctic islands, including Iceland.
Similar Species: the Red Fox (*Vulpes vulpes*), which is larger and usually more rufous.

short
bob-tail

raccoon-like
face mask

right
fore

left
hind

The Raccoon-like Dog is about the same size as the Red Fox, but is rather shaggy and more stockily built, and has a short bushy tail. It occurs in a wide variety of habitats, and feeds on almost any small animal as well as fruits and other plant matter. The footprints are dog-like, but more rounded than a fox's, and the trails are often interrupted, not continuous like those of a fox.
Range: originally from eastern Asia, the Raccoon-like Dog was introduced into the USSR in the 20th century and has also escaped from fur farms. Within Europe its range is spreading and it is now widespread in eastern Europe.
Similar Species: the Feral Dog (*Canis familiaris*) and the Red Fox (*Vulpes vulpes*), which have longer tails. The Raccoon (*Procyon lotor*) has a similar facial pattern, but is distinguished by its longer, banded tail.

	RACCOON-LIKE DOG
Type	dog
Habitat	very variable
Status	feral; spreading its range in Europe

	PHYSICAL DETAILS
Head & Body	50–80cm
Tail	10–26cm
Weight	3–10kg
Teeth	3.1.4.2
	3.1.4.3
Colour	greyish, with darker legs and dark face mask

	FOOD AND HABITS
Food	rodents, amphibians, vegetable matter
Nest	dens with 2 or more entrances, up to 2m deep
Behaviour	mainly nocturnal
Voice	unknown
Hibernation	becomes torpid in winter, but does not hibernate for long
Migration	none

	LIFE CYCLE
Litters	1 a year; summer
Young	usually 5–8, up to 19; blind and helpless
Maturity	8–11 months
Longevity	over 10 years in captivity, less in wild

Stoat *Mustela erminea*

winter

partially moulted

black tip

summer

STOAT
Type weasel
Habitat ubiquitous
Status not threatened

PHYSICAL DETAILS
Head & Body 17.5–31cm
Tail 5.7–14cm
Weight 95–445g
Teeth $\frac{3.1.3.1}{3.1.3.2}$
Colour brown above; creamy white below; black-tipped tail

FOOD AND HABITS
Food mostly small mammals
Nest in rodent burrows, rock piles
Behaviour diurnal and nocturnal
Voice squeaks and chatters
Hibernation none
Migration none

LIFE CYCLE
Litters 1 a year; early summer
Young 6–12; blind, with white fur
Maturity year following birth
Longevity c7 years in wild

The Stoat is one of the most common and widespread predators in Europe, absent only from the south. It is dark, reddish brown above and creamy white below, with a black-tipped tail. In the northern parts of their range (including Britain) they turn white in winter, except for the black tip to their tail. This pelage is the ermine used to trim regalia of European monarchy. In Ireland, where Weasels (*M. nivalis*) are absent, Stoats are smaller than those from the British mainland. They feed on mammals up to the size of small rabbits. Stoats (and Weasels) can be attracted by making squeaking noises.
Range: most of Europe except the Mediterranean region.
Similar Species: most likely confused with the Weasel (*M. nivalis*), which is smaller and lacks the black tail tip.

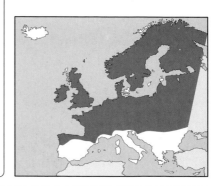

winter
(north of
range only)

left
fore

right
hind

The smallest European carnivore, the Weasel varies in size more than almost any other mammal. In the north of its continental range it is often not much larger than the mice and voles that form its main prey, but in the south it is as large as a Stoat (which does not occur in most of the Mediterranean region). Weasels are prolific, in some areas breeding almost all the year round. Many books record a pygmy weasel, but this is just the smaller form, the young of the late litters, often from females born that year. In Scandinavia and Russia, Weasels turn white in winter.
Range: occurs throughout Europe, except Ireland, Crete, Iceland and a few other islands.
Similar Species: only likely to be confused with the Stoat (*M. erminea*), which is larger, with a proportionally longer, black-tipped tail.

WEASEL

Type	weasel
Habitat	almost all terrrestrial habitats
Status	not threatened

PHYSICAL DETAILS

Head & Body	11–26cm
Tail	17–87mm
Weight	30–200g
Teeth	$\frac{3.1.3.1}{3.1.3.2}$
Colour	reddish brown above; white below; some turn white in winter

FOOD AND HABITS

Food	mostly voles, and mice
Nest	in rodent burrow
Behaviour	diurnal and nocturnal
Voice	squeaks and chitters
Hibernation	none
Migration	none

LIFE CYCLE

Litters	1 or 2 a year; summer
Young	usually 4–6, up to 12; blind with white fur
Maturity	4 months
Longevity	up to 8 years

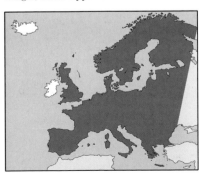

European Mink *Mustela lutreola*

dropping

often white on upper lip, sometimes asymmetrical

white usually confined to lower lip

M. lutreola

M. vison

left hind

left fore

	EUROPEAN MINK
Type	weasel
Habitat	mostly wetlands, including reedbeds, rivers and lakes
Status	endangered

	PHYSICAL DETAILS
Head & Body	28–43cm
Tail	12–19cm
Weight	550–800g
Teeth	$\frac{3.1.3.1}{3.1.3.2}$
Colour	blackish brown

	FOOD AND HABITS
Food	mostly small animals; also fish
Nest	burrow in bank or hollow tree
Behaviour	crepuscular and nocturnal
Voice	chatters
Hibernation	none
Migration	none

	LIFE CYCLE
Litters	1 a year; spring
Young	3–7; blind and helpless
Maturity	year following birth
Longevity	up to 10 years

The European Mink is normally dark blackish brown, with a small amount of white on the muzzle, and occasionally on the throat. It is very similar to the domesticated mink, which is descended from the American Mink (*M. vison*), and occurs ferally in Europe. The range of the European mink is contracting, and it is now extinct or endangered throughout its European range.
Range: occurs in two populations; one in western France, and possibly northwestern Spain; the other in eastern Europe from Romania north to Finland.
Similar Species: the American Mink is slightly larger and often has white fur on the lower lip only. The Otter (*Lutra lutra*) is much larger, with a longer tail, while aquatic rodents – the Coypu (*Myocastor coypus*), the Muskrat (*Ondatra zibethicus*), water voles and rats – do not swim with the same agility.

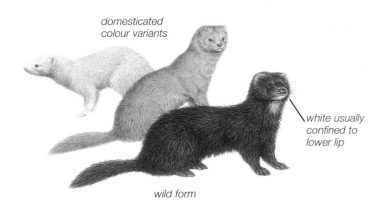

domesticated
colour variants

white usually
confined to
lower lip

wild form

The American Mink occurs ferally in many parts of Europe, having escaped from fur farms. It is, on average, 60 per cent larger than the European Mink (*M. lutreola*), and can often be distinguished from that species by having a small amount of white confined to the lower lip; if there is white on the upper lip it is usually less extensive than in the European Mink. The American Mink has been bred in a wide variety of colours and these variants may turn up in the wild. It has been alleged to displace the European Mink where the ranges overlap, but there is little evidence for this, and the European Mink was declining prior to the arrival of the American.

Range: widespread in Scandinavia and eastwards to Russia; also occurs in the British Isles.

Similar Species: European Mink.

AMERICAN MINK	
Type	weasel
Habitat	mostly near water
Status	feral; range increasing; often considered a pest

PHYSICAL DETAILS	
Head & Body	31–45cm
Tail	12–25cm
Weight	0.4–1.5kg
Teeth	$\frac{3.1.3.1}{3.1.3.2}$
Colour	blackish

FOOD AND HABITS	
Food	wide variety, including fish, small mammals, amphibians, birds, invertebrates
Nest	den among roots or in burrows
Behaviour	mostly crepuscular and nocturnal
Voice	hisses, chitters
Hibernation	none
Migration	none

LIFE CYCLE	
Litters	1 a year; early summer
Young	3–6, blind and helpless
Maturity	year following birth
Longevity	10+ years

Polecat *Mustela putorius*

Ferret
(dark form)

Ferret
(albino form)

face mask

dark back

M. putorius

POLECAT
Type weasel
Habitat variable, but mostly woodland; often close to human settlements
Status threatened and exploited, but protected and increasing

PHYSICAL DETAILS
Head & Body 29–46cm
Tail 8.5–21cm
Weight 0.4–1.7kg
Teeth $\frac{3.1.3.1}{3.1.3.2}$
Colour creamy, with dark brown guard hairs

FOOD AND HABITS
Food small mammals, birds, invertebrates
Nest unknown
Behaviour mostly nocturnal
Voice hisses, chitters, growls
Hibernation none
Migration none

LIFE CYCLE
Litters 1 a year; summer
Young 2–12; blind, almost naked
Maturity in second year
Longevity up to 15 years in captivity, less in wild

The Polecat is closely related to the Domestic Ferret, which it resembles in build. Its creamy yellow underfur shows through the longer, dark brown guard hairs. The facial mask is also characteristic. Polecats have a strong, unpleasant smell, which is used to mark territory. Although it has been hunted and exterminated as a pest, the Polecat is now protected and numbers are increasing.
Range: widespread over most of Europe except the far north, the southern Balkans and most islands.
Similar Species: the Domestic Ferret, which occurs as an escape is usually paler with a larger face band, but since the two interbreed, it can be impossible to distinguish them. Mink are darker and lack the face mask. The Steppe Polecat (*M. eversmannii*) and the Marbled Polecat (*Vormela peregusna*) are paler.

pale back

face mask

A pale-coloured polecat with a darker underside. It feeds on small animals and the mounds of food remains and excrement near the entrances to its burrows have a distinctive and unpleasant smell.

Range: considerably fragmented; it occurs sporadically from Austria and Hungary eastwards through Romania, Slovakia, eastern Germany and Poland, only becoming more widespread in Russia and the Ukraine.

Similar Species: the Polecat (*M. putorius*), of which it is considered by some to be a subspecies. The Steppe Polecat is almost identical in size and structure, but the fur on its back is paler. It is very similar to the Domestic Ferret, and may be an ancestor. The Steppe Polecat can be distinguished from ground squirrels by its dark belly.

STEPPE POLECAT

Type	weasel
Habital	grasslands and steppes
Status	rare in Europe; exploited for fur

PHYSICAL DETAILS

Head & Body	29–46cm
Tail	7–16cm
Weight	up to 960g
Teeth	3.1.3.1
	3.1.3.2
Colour	pale brownish above, darker below

FOOD AND HABITS

Food	rodents
Nest	in burrow
Behaviour	crepuscular or nocturnal
Voice	unknown
Hibernation	none
Migration	occasional mass movements in times of food shortage

LIFE CYCLE

Litters	1 a year; summer
Young	usually 8–11, up to 18; blind and helpless
Maturity	10 months
Longevity	5–6 years in wild

Marbled Polecat *Vormela peregusna*

heavily
mottled back

variety of dorsal
pelage patterns

MARBLED POLECAT

Type	weasel
Habitat	dry, open areas
Status	rare

PHYSICAL DETAILS

Head & Body	27–35cm
Tail	12–18cm
Weight	370–715g
Teeth	$\frac{3.1.3.1}{3.1.3.2}$
Colour	creamy brown with dark markings above; blackish brown below

FOOD AND HABITS

Food	rodents and other small animals
Nest	burrow
Behaviour	mostly crepuscular
Voice	growls
Hibernation	none
Migration	none

LIFE CYCLE

Litters	1 a year; summer
Young	4–8; blind and helpless
Maturity	year following birth
Longevity	probably c10 years

In size and shape the Marbled Polecat is similar to other polecats, but more strikingly marked. The upperparts are creamy brown with a very variable pattern of dark brown marbling, and the tail is tipped with dark brown or black. The underparts are uniformly dark, and the face markings are similar to those of other polecats. The Marbled Polecat is found in dry grasslands, saltmarshes, steppes and farmlands, at altitudes of up to 2100m. Recent studies indicate that this species is more closely related to the martens than other polecats.
Range: restricted to the extreme southeast and the Ukraine.
Similar Species: other polecats—see above. The Beech Marten (*Martes foina*) is larger and darker. Ground squirrels lack dark markings.

left
fore

yellowish throat

left
hind

dropping

bushy tail

A cat-sized carnivore, rich brown above, with an irregularly shaped yellowish throat patch. Pine Martens are normally found in well-wooded habitats, where they are agile climbers. They feed on small mammals and birds, also berries and fruits. Although generally nocturnal and shy, when not persecuted they are seen by day. They have a bounding gait. The droppings are often left on rocks or logs as territory markers.

Range: widespread over most of Europe, but has been exterminated in much of Britain, surviving in Scotland, and in a few isolated populations in England, Wales and Ireland. Found on Corsica, Sardinia and Sicily as well as several Scottish and Scandinavian islands.

Similar Species: the Beech Marten (*M. foina*), which is white below. Mink and polecats are both smaller with less prominent ears.

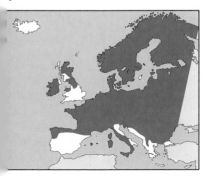

PINE MARTEN

Type	weasel
Habitat	woodlands, forest
Status	locally rare; extinct in some areas

PHYSICAL DETAILS

Head & Body	35–58cm
Tail	17–28cm
Weight	0.5–1.8kg
Teeth	$\frac{3.1.4.1}{3.1.4.2}$
Colour	brown above, with a yellowish throat and belly

FOOD AND HABITS

Food	birds and small mammals
Nest	among rocks, in tree hole or old squirrel drey, or bird nest box
Behaviour	mostly crepuscular
Voice	usually silent; occasional growls or squeals
Hibernation	none
Migration	none, but may wander extensively in winter

LIFE CYCLE

Litters	1 a year; spring
Young	2–7, usually 3; blind and helpless, covered with pale fur
Maturity	about 5 months
Longevity	up to 18 years

Beech Marten *Martes foina*

white throat
(often very
small patch)

BEECH MARTEN

Type	weasel
Habitat	woodland, scrub, rocky hillsides
Status	locally a pest

PHYSICAL DETAILS

Head & Body	44–54cm
Tail	23–32cm
Weight	1.1–2.1kg
Teeth	$\frac{3.1.4.1}{3.1.4.2}$
Colour	brown above, with white throat

FOOD AND HABITS

Food	mammals, birds and other small animals
Nest	in burrows, among rocks
Behaviour	mostly crepuscular; also diurnal
Voice	probably growls, but generally silent
Hibernation	none
Migration	none

LIFE CYCLE

Litters	1 a year; spring
Young	1–8; blind and helpless
Maturity	1–2 years
Longevity	up to 14 years

The Beech Marten is very similar in size and general appearance to the Pine Marten (*M. martes*), but is slightly more heavily built and has a pure white throat patch, which is usually smaller than in that species. Also known as the Stone Marten the Beech Marten is found in more arid, open and often rocky habitats than the Pine Marten, up to 2400m, often above the tree-line. Beech Martens are frequently found close to human habitation, and in a few areas occur in suburbs of towns, where they feed on rats, mice, sparrows and occasionally domestic fowl. In some areas they cause damage in buildings. *Range:* widespread throughout much of Europe, but absent from most of Scandinavia and the British Isles. Occurs on Crete, Rhodes, Corfu and other islands. *Similar Species:* the Pine Marten has a yellowish throat.

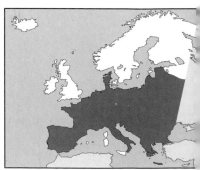

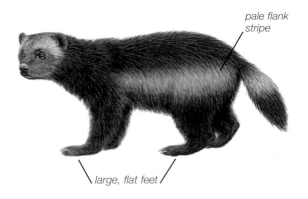

pale flank stripe

large, flat feet

The Wolverine is a large, almost bear- or badger-like relative of the weasels. It is dark brown with a distinctive pale stripe across the flanks. Also known as the Glutton, this animal is omnivorous and a predator. It is capable of bringing down reindeer and other large mammals.

Range: formerly more widespread in Europe, occurring as far south and west as Germany, the Wolverine is now confined to arctic Scandinavia and Russia, and is rare even within these areas. It occurs throughout the Arctic, in both the Old and the New World.

Similar Species: unlikely to be confused with any other species except possibly the Pine Marten (*Martes martes*), which is smaller and more slender, and the Brown Bear (*Ursus arctos*), which is much larger.

WOLVERINE	
Type	weasel
Habitat	forest, tundra
Status	endangered

PHYSICAL DETAILS	
Head & Body	70–86cm
Tail	13–25cm
Weight	up to 32kg
Teeth	$\frac{3.1.4.1}{3.1.4.2}$
Colour	dark brown, paler on flanks

FOOD AND HABITS	
Food	omnivorous
Nest	den amongst tree roots or in snowdrift
Behaviour	nocturnal and diurnal
Voice	unknown
Hibernation	none
Migration	in north, migrates south

LIFE CYCLE	
Litters	1 a year; late winter–spring
Young	2–3; helpless, covered with white fur
Maturity	second year
Longevity	17+ years in captivity, less in wild

Otter *Lutra Lutra*

left fore

right hind

spraint

spraint

blunt muzzle

tapering tail

OTTER

Type	otter
Habitat	wetlands, rivers and coasts
Status	rare or endangered in most of range

PHYSICAL DETAILS

Head & Body	68–80cm
Tail	35–47cm
Weight	up to 15kg
Teeth	3.1.4.1
	3.1.3.2
Colour	dark brown above, paler below

FOOD AND HABITS

Food	mostly aquatic animals, particularly fish
Nest	holt, usually among tree roots
Behaviour	mostly nocturnal
Voice	whistles, squeaks, chitters
Hibernation	none
Migration	none but wanders widely

LIFE CYCLE

Litters	1 a year; at almost any time of year, but not midwinter in north
Young	1–5; furred, but blind and helpless
Maturity	2nd or 3rd year
Longevity	up to c20 years

Most likely to be seen in or near water, the Otter is superbly adapted to swimming. It is streamlined, has webbed feet, and its glossy fur is water-resistant. The droppings are usually left on a promontory or by a bridge. They have a sweet smell and often contain fish scales. Because of persecution, Otters are usually nocturnal and shy.
Range: formerly widespread and abundant across Europe the Otter is now extremely rare or extinct over most of its range, only occuring in any numbers in Scandinavia, Scotland and Ireland.
Similar Species: Otters are frequently misidentified – usually the species turns out to be the American Mink (*Mustela vison*), the Coypu (*Myocastor coypus*) or the Muskrat (*Ondatra zibethicus*), all of which are smaller and more heavily built, and swim more slowly.

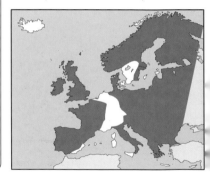

stranded hairs

right fore

left hind

black and white face

short legs

An unmistakable animal, coloured grey above and black below, and with a distinctive black and white face. Badgers are usually nocturnal and shy, but occasionally visit gardens to be fed. They are sometimes seen in car headlights, and can be observed by watching their burrows or setts from downwind. The setts are often extensive with several entrances, which measure about 20cm in diameter. They may be used for many decades resulting in large spoil heaps around the entrances. Well marked paths lead to feeding grounds (often pastures), scratching trees and latrine pits.
Range: occurs over most of Europe except extreme north, and some islands.
Similar Species: not likely to be confused with any other species.

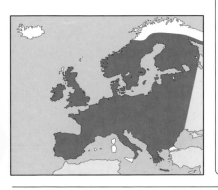

BADGER

Type	badger
Habitat	mostly woodlands near pastures
Status	not threatened, but persecuted in some areas

PHYSICAL DETAILS

Head & Body	67–87cm
Tail	11–19cm
Weight	8.7–17.3kg; occasionally 30+kg
Teeth	$\underline{3.1.3.1}$ 3.1.3.2
Colour	grey above, black below; distinctive head markings

FOOD AND HABITS

Food	omnivorous; earthworms important
Nest	sett, comprising labyrinth of tunnels; nest lined with grasses
Behaviour	mostly crepuscular and nocturnal, but occasionally diurnal
Voice	wide range of growls, barks, purrs, etc.
Hibernation	none; stays in sett during cold weather
Migration	none

LIFE CYCLE

Litters	1 a year; late winter–early spring
Young	1–5; blind and helpless
Maturity	1–2 years
Longevity	up to 15 years

Egyptian Mongoose *Herpestes ichneumon*

pointed snout

tapering tail

EGYPTIAN MONGOOSE

Type	mongoose
Habitat	thick scrub, rocky hillsides
Status	not threatened; protected in Spain

PHYSICAL DETAILS

Head & Body	50–65cm
Tail	35–55cm
Weight	4–8kg
Teeth	<u>3.1.3</u> or <u>4.1–3</u> 3.1.3 or 4.1–3
Colour	greyish brown

FOOD AND HABITS

Food	omnivore; mostly small animals; eggs
Nest	usually in rock cleft or burrow
Behaviour	mostly nocturnal
Voice	probably growls, hisses, but mostly silent
Hibernation	none
Migration	none

LIFE CYCLE

Litters	1 a year; early spring
Young	up to 4; blind and helpless
Maturity	2nd year
Longevity	5–7 years

The Egyptian Mongoose is similar in build to a marten, but is larger and more slender, and has a tapering tail. The coat is greyish and rather coarse. This animal is found in arid, rocky areas with thick scrub.
Range: introduced into Europe from North Africa, and found in Spain and Portugal.
Similar Species: the Polecat (*Mustela putorius*), which is smaller, with a face mask and a short, thin tail; the Beech Marten (*Martes foina*), which is a richer brown, smaller and has a whitish throat and a thinner tail; the Genet (*Genetta genetta*), which is heavily spotted. The Indian Grey Mongoose (*H. edwardsi*), introduced into Italy, is smaller and greyer than the Egyptian *H. auropunctatus* has been introduced in the eastern Adriatic where it is common.

right fore

left hind

face mask

banded tail

At close quarters the Raccoon is unlikely to be mistaken for any other species, except perhaps the Raccoon-like Dog (*Nyctereutus procynoides*). The rather rounded appearance, banded tail and 'robber's mask' are characteristic. Usually crepuscular or nocturnal, Raccoons are often seen close to water, frequently with their young. They are generally slow moving, but gallop away when alarmed, and often take to trees. When abundant, Raccoons are often killed on roads.

Range: native of North America, the Raccoon was introduced into Europe for its fur, and now occurs over a wide area and is spreading. The two main centres of its distribution are in western Germany and around the Baltic states.

Similar Species: the Raccoon-like Dog – see above.

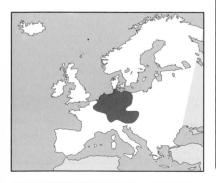

RACCOON
Type	raccoon
Habitat	mostly woodlands, near water
Status	introduced; range spreading

PHYSICAL DETAILS
Head & Body	60–95cm
Tail	19–40cm
Weight	5.5–21.6kg
Teeth	3.1.4.2
	3.1.4.2
Colour	grey with distinctive black face mask and banded tail

FOOD AND HABITS
Food	omnivore
Nest	den and breeding nest, usually in hollow tree
Behaviour	nocturnal
Voice	varied; snarls, hisses, screams, growls
Hibernation	none, but may sleep for several days
Migration	none

LIFE CYCLE
Litters	1 a year; spring
Young	1–7; blind and helpless
Maturity	less than 6 months
Longevity	up to 14 years in captivity, less in wild

Lynx *Lynx lynx*

short tail

L. lynx

ear tufts

right fore

left hind

L. pardina

long legs

LYNX
Type cat
Habitat forests and scrub
Status rare and endangered; hunted for pelt

PHYSICAL DETAILS
Head & Body 80–130cm
Tail 13–30cm
Weight up to 32kg
Teeth $\frac{3.1.2.1}{3.1.2.1}$
Colour sandy to greyish, with spotting (sometimes prominent); paler in winter

FOOD AND HABITS
Food carnivorous; principally birds and mammals
Nest lair in hollow tree or rock cleft
Behaviour nocturnal and diurnal
Voice purrs, growls
Hibernation none
Migration wanders during food shortages

LIFE CYCLE
Litters 1 a year; early summer
Young 1–4; furred, but blind and helpless
Maturity 2nd year
Longevity up to 18 years in captivity, less in wild

A large cat with a short tail and prominent ear tufts. The amount of spotting is variable, the most heavily spotted animals coming from Spain and the Carpathians. The endangered Iberian population is now usually regarded as a separate species (*L. pardina*). The Lynx feeds on a wide range of mostly warm-blooded prey; large animals are suffocated with a bite in the throat.
Range: although it is now extinct over much of Europe, there have been several successful reintroductions, and its range is spreading. The Spanish population, however, is continuing to decline.
Similar Species: only likely to be confused with the Wild Cat (*Felis sylvestris*) and the Domestic Cat (*F. catus*), both of which are smaller, with proportionally longer tails.

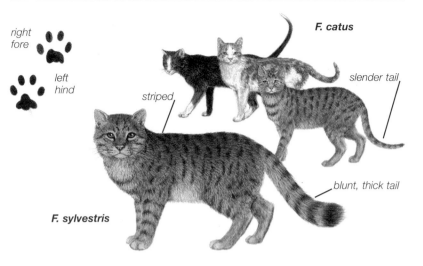

right
fore

left
hind

F. catus

striped

slender tail

blunt, thick tail

F. sylvestris

There is still much confusion concerning Wild Cats in Europe. Although the populations in Scotland are distinctively different from Feral and Domestic Cats (*F. catus*), those in the Mediterranean are less so. At one time the populations on the islands of Corsica, Sardinia and Majorca were considered to be a different species (*F. lybica*) but all are now treated as a single species.

Range: although its range is considerably reduced, it is apparently spreading in France as well as Scotland. Its status in Corsica, the Balearics and other islands is uncertain.

Similar Species: Feral and Domestic Cats (*F. catus*), particularly mackerel tabbies. The Wild Cat can best be distinguished by its tail shape – Domestic and Feral Cats with wild-type patterning have more tapering tails.

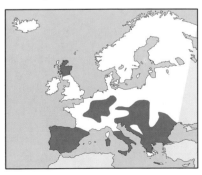

	WILD CAT
Type	cat
Habitat	forests, woodlands, scrub and more open rocky habitats in south
Status	probably increasing in most parts of its range, where there are suitable habitats remaining

PHYSICAL DETAILS

Head & Body	51–75cm
Tail	23–36cm
Weight	up to 7kg
Teeth	$\frac{3.1.3.1}{3.1.2.1}$
Colour	tabby, similar to domestic version

FOOD AND HABITS

Food	mammals, birds and other small animals
Nest	lair among rocks, under logs
Behaviour	mostly nocturnal
Voice	similar to Domestic Cat
Hibernation	none
Migration	none

LIFE CYCLE

Litters	1 a year; early summer; occasionally 2nd or 3rd litters later in year
Young	1–8; blind and helpless
Maturity	year after birth
Longevity	13–14 years

Genet *Genetta genetta*

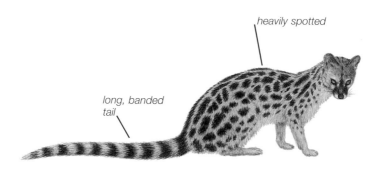

heavily spotted

long, banded tail

	GENET
Type	cat-like
Habitat	scrub, woodland and open, but well-vegetated habitats
Status	not threatened; protected and increasing

	PHYSICAL DETAILS
Head & Body	47–60cm
Tail	40–51cm
Weight	1.3–2.4g
Teeth	$\frac{3.1.4.2}{3.1.4.2}$
Colour	sandy yellow, dense spots, heavily banded tail

	FOOD AND HABITS
Food	birds, small mammals
Nest	lair in hollow tree, rock cleft or among roots
Behaviour	nocturnal
Voice	relatively silent; miaows and hisses
Hibernation	none
Migration	none

	LIFE CYCLE
Litters	1 a year; early spring or late summer
Young	1–3; blind and helpless
Maturity	2–4 years
Longevity	up to 13 years in captivity, less in wild

The Genet is a slender, cat-like carnivore, heavily spotted with a long, heavily banded tail and prominent ears. A nocturnal animal, it is rarely seen. It was introduced into Europe from North Africa, where it was probably once domesticated.

Range: widespread from the Iberian peninsula west through most of France, where its range is spreading. It also occurs on Majorca.

Similar Species: only likely to be confused with the Wild Cat (*Felis sylvestris*) and the Domestic Cat (*Felis catus*), which have much shorter tails and proportionally longer legs.

concave face

head profile

small size

'v'-shaped nostrils

buff-brown

This small seal is often seen in and around estuaries, and may travel inland, swimming up rivers. Its muzzle is concave. Common Seals breed in midsummer, so are prone to disturbance from humans. The pups are often born on sand bars or rocks, so have to swim within a few hours of birth. These seals are gregarious, hauling out in groups of up to 100 or more.

Range: widespread in the North Sea, around the British Isles, south to northern Spain, and north to Arctic Scandinavia and Iceland.

Similar Species: most likely to be confused with the Grey Seal (*Halichoerus grypus*), which is larger and has a characteristic 'Roman nose'. The Ringed Seal (*P. hispida*), is very similar in size and profile to the Common, but has a distinctive pattern of rings on its back.

COMMON SEAL

Type	seal
Habitat	coastal marine
Status	declining in many areas; protected through most of Europe

PHYSICAL DETAILS

Length	1.2–1.6m
Weight	up to 150kg
Teeth	$\frac{3.1.5}{2.1.5}$
Colour	mottled greys and browns

FOOD AND HABITS

Food	mostly fish
Behaviour	mostly diurnal
Voice	pups have wailing call, but otherwise generally silent
Hibernation	none
Migration	disperses from breeding grounds

LIFE CYCLE

Litters	1 a year; midsummer
Young	1; active from birth
Maturity	2–6 years
Longevity	up to 30 years

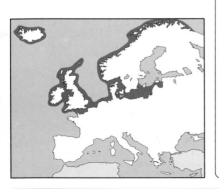

Ringed Seal *Phoca hispida*

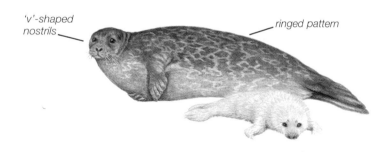

'v'-shaped nostrils

ringed pattern

RINGED SEAL	
Type	seal
Habitat	marine; landlocked lakes
Status	declining in Europe; several isolated populations endangered

PHYSICAL DETAILS	
Length	1.35–1.85m
Weight	90–110kg
Teeth	$\frac{2-3.1.4-6}{1-2.1.4-5}$
Colour	greyish brown, with ring patterning

FOOD AND HABITS	
Food	fish
Nest	may make protective hollow in snow for pup
Behaviour	both diurnal and nocturnal
Voice	unknown
Hibernation	none
Migration	disperses from breeding grounds

LIFE CYCLE	
Litters	1; early spring; on ice
Young	1; covered with white fur; active from birth
Maturity	7–8 years
Longevity	up to 40 years

A small seal that is similar in general appearance to the Common Seal (*P. vitulina*), but generally slightly darker with a characteristic pattern of rings on its back. In the winter it often lives beneath the ice, keeping holes open for breathing. The pups are born on the ice, often in a hollow in a snow drift, during early spring, and do not shed their thick white fur until they are 2–4 weeks old.

Range: one of the few seals to occur in fresh water, being found in land-locked lakes in the Gulf of Finland, such as Lake Saimaa and Lake Lagoda. They are also found in the Baltic and in Arctic waters.

Similar Species: most likely to be confused with the Common Seal, which has less clearly defined markings; most other seals are larger.

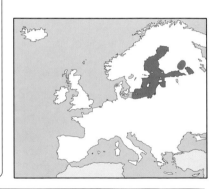

Halichoerus grypus # Grey Seal

'Roman' nose

♂ head profile

dog-like head

♀

A large seal with a wide range in Europe. It has a distinctive dog-like head, with a convex profile. The male is usually dark with light blotches; the female pale with dark blotches. The young are born with a yellowish coat, which they moult when a month old. Grey Seals make a wide range of barking calls, and when fully adult, have a wailing song. They are gregarious, often hauling out in densely packed groups. *Range:* most abundant around the British Isles, though ranging from northern Iberia to the Baltic, around Scandinavia to Russia, the Baltic Republics and Iceland. *Similar Species:* the Common Seal (*Phoca vitulina*) which is smaller, and has a concave face. In the north of its range the Hooded (*Cystophora cristata*) and Bearded (*Erignathus barbatus*) Seals overlap and are a similar size.

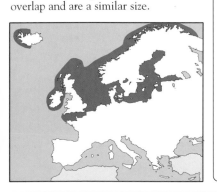

GREY SEAL

Type	seal
Habitat	marine, breeding on shore
Status	protected; increasing in some areas, decreasing in others

PHYSICAL DETAILS

Length	1.65–2.3m
Weight	105–310kg
Teeth	$\frac{3.1.5 \text{ or } 6}{2.1.5}$
Colour	variable, often greyish with blotches

FOOD AND HABITS

Food	fish
Nest	none
Behaviour	mostly diurnal on breeding grounds
Voice	very varied, includes barks, bleats, moans
Hibernation	none
Migration	wanders extensively outside breeding season

LIFE CYCLE

Litters	1; autumn; on shore
Young	1; covered with white fur; active from birth
Maturity	4–10 years
Longevity	up to 46 years

Monk Seal *Monachus monachus*

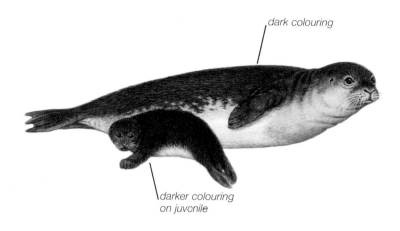

dark colouring

darker colouring
on juvenile

MONK SEAL	
Type	seal
Habitat	marine
Status	endangered
PHYSICAL DETAILS	
Length	1.9–3.8m
Weight	260–300kg
Teeth	$\frac{2.1.5}{2.1.5}$
Colour	dark brown, paler on belly
FOOD AND HABITS	
Food	mainly fish
Behaviour	diurnal and nocturnal
Voice	barks, howls, yelps, 'sneezes'
Hibernation	none
Migration	disperses from breeding sites
LIFE CYCLE	
Litters	1 a year; usually summer or autumn
Young	1; with dark fur; active from birth
Maturity	4 years
Longevity	no data

The only seal found in the Mediterranean, and therefore unlikely to be confused with any other species. It is generally dark brown above, often with a paler patch on the belly. Monk seals are generally extremely shy and breed on remote beaches on uninhabited islands, or in sea caves. The pup is dark chocolate-brown at birth and remains on shore until it is about 6 weeks old. These seals are often very vocal, with a wide range of barks, howls, dog-like yelps, and 'sneezes'.
Range: virtually extinct in the western Mediterranean, and extremely localized in the eastern Mediterranean. One of the largest populations survives in the Northern Sporades, in the Aegean Sea.
Similar Species: other seals, but their ranges do not normally overlap that of the Monk Seal; dolphins and porpoises have dorsal fins.

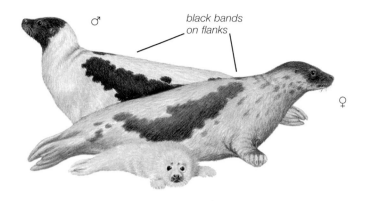

black bands
on flanks

♂

♀

A medium-sized seal, found mostly in the Arctic. Like all seals, it is difficult to identify at sea, but adult males are distinctive. They are creamy white with a blackish head and a characteristic blackish marking across the back – the 'harp'. The females have a washed out version of the males' markings. Harp Seals breed in large colonies on pack ice, migrating north as the ice retreats in summer. They are gregarious for most of the year.

Range: breeds around northern Scandinavia and Russia. Outside the breeding season the colonies disperse, and occasionally wander south as far as Britain and western Sweden.

Similar Species: other seals lack the distinctive markings of the male Harp, but immatures are very similar to the Ringed Seal (*Phoca hispida*) and the Common Seal (*P. vitulina*).

HARP SEAL

Type	seal
Habitat	marine
Status	not threatened; hunted for skins

PHYSICAL DETAILS

Length	1.8–2m
Weight	100–150kg
Teeth	3.1.4.1 2.1.4.1
Colour	male creamy white with dark head and dark saddle, female less distinctly

FOOD AND HABITS

Food	mostly fish
Nest	none
Behaviour	diurnal
Voice	hoarse bark; pups miaow like cat
Hibernation	none
Migration	disperses after breeding

LIFE CYCLE

Litters	1 a year; on ice; early spring
Young	1; with thick yellowish white fur; active from birth
Maturity	5–6 years
Longevity	30+ years

Bearded Seal *Erignathus barbatus*

sub-adult

long whiskers

adult

BEARDED SEAL

Type	seal
Habitat	marine
Status	stable or possibly declining; hunted

PHYSICAL DETAILS

Length	1.9–2.5m
Weight	225–350kg
Teeth	3.1.4.1
	3.1.4.1
Colour	uniform brownish

FOOD AND HABITS

Food	mainly fish; also invertebrates
Nest	none
Behaviour	mostly diurnal
Voice	high flute-like call, ending in low roar
Hibernation	none
Migration	disperses after breeding

LIFE CYCLE

Litters	1 a year; on ice; spring
Young	1; with grey fur; active from birth
Maturity	5–7 years
Longevity	up to 31 years

A very large seal, with uniform, unspotted colouration, and prominent whiskers. At close quarters each whisker can be seen to end in a tight spiral. The flippers have a characteristic square shape and, as in the Monk Seal (*Monachus monachus*), the females have four nipples. The front flippers are exposed when the seals dive, followed by the hind flippers as they roll forwards. Outside the breeding season, when small aggregations occur, they are solitary. Bearded Seals feed almost exclusively on slow-moving fish and invertebrates found on the sea bed.
Range: circumpolar; only rarely seen further south, mostly in the northern part of the North Sea.
Similar Species: other seals, but most have some spotting, blotches or other markings.

nasal sac (or bladder inflated)

♂ displays

'hood' inflated

♂

♀

juvenile

A large seal, coloured greyish with light spots, some of which join together to form pale rings around darker blotches. The female is generally less clearly marked than the male. A distinctive feature of the male is the nasal crest, which can be inflated to form a large, football-sized bladder. Beached animals can be identified by the presence of only a single lower canine on each side of the jaw, and widely spaced, peg-like post-canines. The pups moult into blue-grey fur soon after birth and become independent at about one month.
Range: breeds on Jan Mayan, near Spitzbergen, and disperses south to Arctic Norway, Iceland and Spitzbergen; vagrants occur south as far as Britain.
Similar Species: other seals, particularly the Grey Seal (*Halichoerus grypus*), which has a more pointed head; also, the male lacks a bladder.

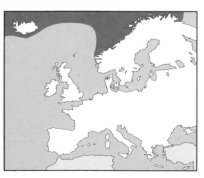

HOODED SEAL

Type	seal
Habitat	marine
Status	over-hunted in many areas

PHYSICAL DETAILS

Length	1.8–2.5m
Weight	up to 400kg
Teeth	2.1.4.1 / 1.1.4.1
Colour	grey with blotches above, whitish below

FOOD AND HABITS

Food	squid and fish
Nest	none
Behaviour	mostly diurnal
Voice	roars and bellows
Hibernation	none
Migration	disperses south after breeding

LIFE CYCLE

Litters	1 a year; early spring
Young	1; with white fur; active from birth
Maturity	3–4 years
Longevity	up to 35 years

Walrus *Odobenus rosmarus*

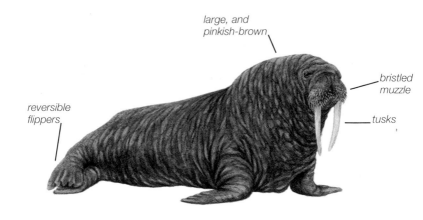

large, and pinkish-brown

bristled muzzle

tusks

reversible flippers

WALRUS

Type	seal
Habitat	marine
Status	formerly threatened but possibly recovering

PHYSICAL DETAILS

Length	up to 2.5m
Weight	up to 1.2 tonnes
Teeth	$\frac{1.1.3}{0.1.3}$
Colour	greyish

FOOD AND HABITS

Food	mainly bivalve molluscs; occasionally seals
Nest	none
Behaviour	mainly diurnal
Voice	grunts, barks
Hibernation	none
Migration	disperses to breeding grounds

LIFE CYCLE

Litters	1; on ice or rocky shores; early summer
Young	1; active from birth
Maturity	4–7 years
Longevity	c40 years

The largest seal in European waters, coloured uniform grey or yellowish, or pinkish grey, with prominent bristles on the upper lip. The males and some females have large (up to 1m) tusks. On land the feet point forward, unlike the feet of other European seals. Walruses are usually found close to Arctic ice, where they feed by diving for molluscs, staying underwater for up to 10 minutes. They breed in large herds on the ice in spring and the pups are able to swim within a few hours of birth, but do not become independent for about a year. During the past two centuries walrus populations have been drastically reduced, but may now be recovering slowly.

Range: vagrants occur south to Iceland, Norway and more rarely to Britain.

Similar Species: not likely to be confused with any other seal.

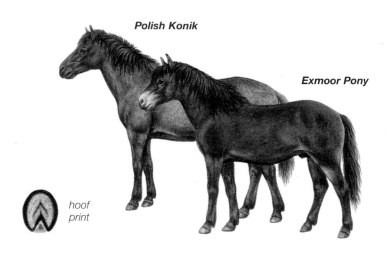

Polish Konik

Exmoor Pony

hoof print

Wild horses or tarpans became extinct in Europe towards the end of the last century. The so-called wild horses and ponies that occur in several parts of Europe are all feral, though some have primitive characteristics. Of them the Exmoor Pony from England is considered the nearest to the wild horse. Most Feral Horses have flowing manes, whereas the original wild horses had erect manes. Since 1936 some herds of 'back-bred' horses, derived from tarpan-like breeds, have been maintained in reserves in Poland.
Range: occurs in Britain and northern Spain, with scattered populations in other parts of Europe.
Similar Species: Feral Donkeys (*E. asinus*) occur occasionally in southern Europe; they are smaller, greyer, have larger ears, and usually have a blackish cross on the shoulders.

FERAL HORSE

Type	horse
Habitat	mountains, moorland
Status	feral; mostly declining

PHYSICAL DETAILS

Head & Body	c2m
Tail	up to 0.5m
Weight	up to 300kg
Teeth	$\frac{3.1.3.3}{3.1.3.3}$
Colour	variable; usually brown

FOOD AND HABITS

Food	grasses, herbage
Nest	none
Behaviour	mostly diurnal
Voice	whinney, neigh
Hibernation	none
Migration	none

LIFE CYCLE

Litters	1, occasionally 2 a year; at almost any time of year
Young	1–2; active from birth
Maturity	2–3 years
Longevity	30+ years in captivity, less in wild

Wild Boar *Sus scrofa*

♂

♀

hoof
prints

young

WILD BOAR

Type	pig
Habitat	ubiquitous; particularly forest, woodland, farmland
Status	depleted, with fragmented range, but locally abundant

PHYSICAL DETAILS

Head & Body	1.1–1.8m
Tail	15–25cm
Weight	50–350kg
Teeth	3.1.4.3 3.1.4.3
Colour	adults greyish brown, young with pale stripes

FOOD AND HABITS

Food	omnivorous
Nest	hollow or depression, usually in dense vegetation; used for giving birth
Behaviour	diurnal and nocturnal
Voice	grunts and squeals
Hibernation	none
Migration	none

LIFE CYCLE

Litters	1 a year; spring
Young	3–12; helpless but develop rapidly and follow the mother
Maturity	in 2nd year
Longevity	up to 20 years

The wild ancestor of the Domestic Pig, the Wild Boar is similar in general shape, but covered with coarse, bristly, dark brown hair. The young have pale longitudinal stripes, and the male has a stiff mane and prominent tusks. Although generally solitary, the young stay with their mothers until well grown, and families may band together in winter. They are often very noisy when rooting in the undergrowth.

Range: widespread over most of Europe, north to southern Scandinavia, extinct in the British Isles by the 18th century, but reintroduced by the 1990s. It is widely hunted and, although it causes damage to agriculture, subject to closed seasons or protection over most of its range.

Similar Species: Domestic Pigs, which sometimes roam freely in woodland, particularly in autumn.

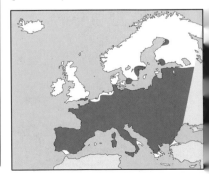

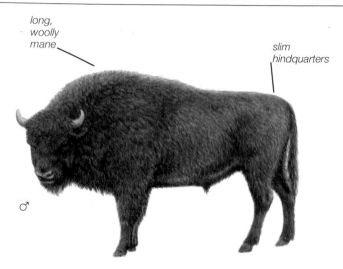

long, woolly mane

slim hindquarters

♂

A massive, cow-like ungulate that is superficially very similar to the American Bison. It has humped shoulders, and is dark brown with long shaggy fur on the forequarters; both sexes carry short, upward-curving horns. The calves are lighter coloured. The Bison was once widespread in European forests, but by the end of the 19th century was confined to Bialowieza Forest on the Polish/Russian border, and the Caucasus. It became extinct in the wild in the early 20th century but survived in private collections and zoos. It lives in herds and browses on leaves, twigs and bark. *Range:* a reintroduced population exists in the Bialowieza Forest, and smaller populations have been introduced into many other reserves in Russia, Poland and Romania.
Similar Species: none.

BISON

Type	cow
Habitat	forest, woodland
Status	confined to reserves

PHYSICAL DETAILS

Head & Body	2.5–3.5m
Tail	50–80cm
Weight	430–850kg
Teeth	0.0.3.3
	3.1.3.3
Colour	dark brown

FOOD AND HABITS

Food	leaves, twigs; other vegetation
Nest	none
Behaviour	mostly diurnal or crepuscular
Voice	moos, bellows
Hibernation	none
Migration	none

LIFE CYCLE

Litters	1 every other year; summer
Young	1; active from birth
Maturity	in 2nd or 3rd year
Longevity	25–30 years

Feral Cattle *Bos taurus*

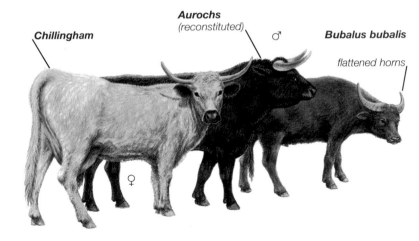

Chillingham

Aurochs
(reconstituted) ♂

Bubalus bubalis

flattened horns

♀

FERAL CATTLE
Type cow
Habitat woodland, parkland, meadows
Status feral; localized

PHYSICAL DETAILS
Head & Body up to c2.5m
Tail up to c50cm
Weight up to 500kg
Teeth $\frac{0.0.3.3}{3.1.3.3}$
Colour white or dark brown; also more variable

FOOD AND HABITS
Food wide range of vegetation
Nest none
Behaviour mostly diurnal
Voice moos, bellows; identical to domesticated cattle
Hibernation none
Migration none

LIFE CYCLE
Litters 1 a year; at any time of year
Young 1, occasionally 2; active from birth
Maturity in 2nd year
Longevity no data

The Wild Ox or Aurochs became extinct in the early 17th century. However, primitive cattle survive in a feral or semi-feral state in several areas. The best known are the white Chillingham cattle, which are confined to parks in Britain. In the Camargue black cattle roam in a semi-feral state. Reconstructed or 'reconstituted' Aurochs have been introduced into the wild in Poland. They are blackish brown, and most primitive cattle have large, out-swept horns.
Range: Britain, France, Spain, Poland, and several Greek islands.
Similar Species: most likely to be confused with domesticated cattle. Bison (*Bison bonasus*) are larger, with shaggy fur. In southern and eastern Europe the Asiatic Water Buffalo (*Bubalus bubalis*) is kept. The flattened horns are backward sweeping.

down-curving horns

long shaggy wool

Unmistakable in the field, the Musk Ox is a large, shaggy relative of the sheep. Both sexes carry broad, downward-curving horns, and below the long outer-fur they have very fine, dense under-fur. They are confined to the arctic, and in winter inhabit windswept hill-tops (where the snow is not deep), moving to valleys and meadows in summer. They are gregarious, living in herds of up to 100. When a herd is threatened by wolves or other predators, the adults form a defensive line or ring, with the calves behind.
Range: by the 1930s the world population had dropped to around 500, all in Canada. The Musk Ox has been introduced in Europe, where it is confined to two areas of northern central Norway and Sweden.
Similar Species: none within range.

MUSK OX

Type	sheep
Habitat	arctic tundra
Status	depleted, with fragmented range

PHYSICAL DETAILS

Head & Body	2–2.5m
Tail	up to c15cm
Weight	180–400kg
Teeth	$\frac{0.0.3.3}{3.1.3.3}$
Colour	grey–brown, with paler areas

FOOD AND HABITS

Food	sedges, grasses, shrubs
Nest	none
Behaviour	mostly diurnal
Voice	unknown
Hibernation	none
Migration	some seasonal movements

LIFE CYCLE

Litters	1; summer
Young	1, occasionally 2; active from birth
Maturity	females 3–4 years, males 6 years
Longevity	25 years

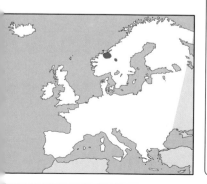

Mouflon *Ovis ammon*

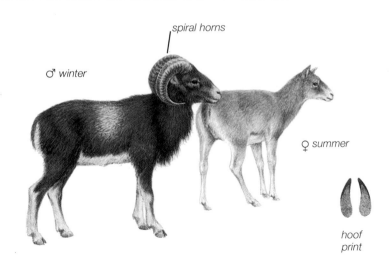

σ' *winter*

spiral horns

♀ *summer*

hoof
print

MOUFLON

Type	sheep
Habitat	mountain grasslands, woodland clearings
Status	has declined, but now substantial numbers in captivity and reserves

PHYSICAL DETAILS

Head & Body	0.8–1.25m
Tail	7–15cm
Weight	20–60kg
Teeth	$\frac{0.0.3.3}{3.1.3.3}$
Horns	males large and coiled; females small or absent
Colour	brown above, pale below with pale patch on sides; males more reddish than females

FOOD AND HABITS

Food	mainly grazes on grass
Nest	none
Behaviour	mostly diurnal, but may be nocturnal in heat of summer
Voice	sheep-like bleat
Hibernation	none
Migration	may descend to lower altitudes in winter

LIFE CYCLE

Litters	1 a year; spring–summer
Young	1 or 2; active from birth
Maturity	females in 1st year, males after 2nd
Longevity	12–15 years

The Mouflon is one of the ancestors of the Domestic Sheep (*O. aries*) and was probably introduced into Europe. Although closely related to the Sheep, its wool is darker and is covered by hair. The adult male carries heavy, curled horns and has a distinctive pale patch on the flanks. The female is paler and the horns are small or absent. Both sexes have a pale rump with a contrasting blackish tail.

Range: the natural range of the Mouflon in Europe was once wide, but its native range is now restricted to Corsica and Sardinia. It has been extensively reintroduced into Europe.

Similar Species: the Domestic Sheep, which occurs throughout the range of the Mouflon. Apart from the differences described above, Domestic Sheep are often most easily recognized by the sound of their bells!

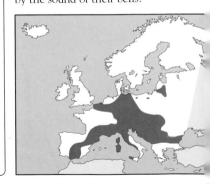

Four-horned ♂

Moorland ♂

Soay ♂

droppings

Since Domestic Sheep are often farmed in remote locations they can be mistaken for wild animals. At close quarters the varieties bred for high wool production are easily identified. Some of the other varieties can be mistaken for Ibex, Chamois, Mouflons or Wild Goats. The easiest way to identify Sheep is often by sound – those in alpine areas frequently have bells. Close up, they are rarely shy and most are woolly. Primitive breeds, such as the Soay Sheep from St Kilda in the Hebrides, occur in several remote areas. *Range:* occurs throughout Europe except the extreme north. *Similar Species:* most likely to be confused with the Mouflon (*O. ammon*), which is darker and generally shyer; and the Wild Goat (*Capra aegagrus*), which has characteristically shaped horns.

DOMESTIC SHEEP

Type	sheep
Habitat	ubiquitous; often in alpine meadows
Status	domesticated

PHYSICAL DETAILS

Head & Body	very variable; up to c1.5m
Tail	often docked, but in some breeds large
Weight	very variable; generally less than 150kg
Teeth	$\frac{0.0.3.3}{3.1.3.3}$
Horns	males coiled, females usually absent
Colour	variable, but often grey or whitish; sometimes variegated

FOOD AND HABITS

Food	grazes mostly on grass
Nest	none
Behaviour	mostly diurnal
Voice	bleats
Hibernation	none
Migration	none; may move down from mountains in winter

LIFE CYCLE

Litters	1 a year; early spring–summer
Young	1–4; fully active from birth
Maturity	in 1st year
Longevity	up to c15 years

Alpine Ibex *Capra ibex*

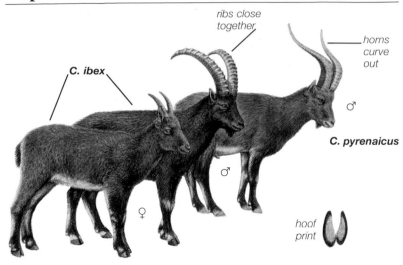

ribs close together

horns curve out

C. ibex

♂

C. pyrenaicus

♀

hoof print

ALPINE IBEX

Type	goat
Habitat	mountains
Status	formerly endangered, but now increasing

PHYSICAL DETAILS

Head & Body	1.15–1.7m
Tail	10–20cm
Weight	35–150kg
Teeth	$\frac{0.0.3.3}{3.1.3.3}$
Horns	both sexes; males larger
Colour	brownish grey

FOOD AND HABITS

Food	mostly grasses; also berries, twigs, bark
Nest	none
Behaviour	mostly diurnal
Voice	normally silent; horn clashing in rut
Hibernation	none
Migration	none; moves down from higher altitudes in winter

LIFE CYCLE

Litters	1 a year; early summer
Young	usually 1, occasionally 2; active from birth
Maturity	in 3rd year
Longevity	12–15 years

An agile goat that lives in precipitous mountain habitats, usually above the tree line. Both sexes carry horns, which in the males can be over 1m long. During the rut the males charge headlong at each other and the clash of their horns can be heard a kilometre away. Outside the rut the males often live in small groups. Females and young form their own groups.
Range: once reduced to a single population in the Gran Paradiso National Park, Italy, but has been reintroduced in the Alps.
Similar Species: the Spanish Ibex (*C. pyrenaicus*) is very similar, differing mainly in horn shape. Its range is quite separate, being confined to isolated mountain groups in Iberia. Domestic Goats (*C. hircus*) in alpine areas can be confused with Ibex but, like Domestic Sheep, usually carry bells.

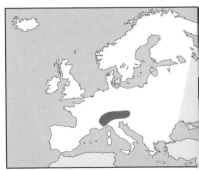

widely spaced ribs

divergent horns

C. hircus

dark shoulder

C. hircus

long hair

♀

droppings

♂

♂♂

C. aegagrus

It is likely that none of the populations of wild goat found in Europe are pure, since they freely interbreed with Domestic Goats. They are also probably all the result of introductions by man. However, a few small populations may be very similar to the truly wild ancestral goat. Wild Goats are generally found in rocky habitats. They browse on shrubs and trees and also graze on a wide variety of grasses and other vegetation.

Range: the most pure-bred populations probably occur on some of the Greek islands, notably Crete and Erimomilos.
Similar Species: Feral Goats (*C. hircus*) occur in many parts of Europe, including many Mediterranean islands and some remote parts of the British Isles. They are often long haired and most have some degree of twisting in their horns.

	WILD GOAT
Type	goat
Habitat	mostly rocky hillsides
Status	rare
	PHYSICAL DETAILS
Head & Body	1.2–1.6m
Tail	15–20cm
Weight	25–40kg
Teeth	$\frac{0.0.3.3}{3.1.3.3}$
Horns	both sexes; males larger
Colour	brown above, paler below, with distinctive blackish stripe down back and around shoulders
	FOOD AND HABITS
Food	wide range of vegetation
Nest	none
Behaviour	diurnal and nocturnal
Voice	generally silent, but occasionally bleats
Hibernation	none
Migration	none
	LIFE CYCLE
Litters	1 a year; spring–autumn
Young	usually 1; fully active within about 4 days
Maturity	1–2 years
Longevity	up to 20 years

Chamois *Rupicapra rupicapra*

black and white face pattern

backward-curving horns

winter

summer

CHAMOIS

Type	goat
Habitat	mountains, near tree-line
Status	threatened in most parts of range

PHYSICAL DETAILS

Head & Body	0.9–1.4m
Tail	3–8cm
Weight	12–50kg
Teeth	$\frac{0.0.3.3}{3.1.3.3}$
Horns	both sexes; small
Colour	reddish brown in summer, blackish in winter; black and white face

FOOD AND HABITS

Food	grasses, herbage; also browses on conifers and other trees
Nest	none
Behaviour	mostly diurnal
Voice	bleats
Hibernation	none
Migration	descends into valleys in winter

LIFE CYCLE

Litters	1 a year; summer
Young	1; active soon after birth
Maturity	3–4 years
Longevity	15–20 years

An agile, goat-like inhabitant of high-altitude pastures. It occurs in isolated populations, generally living above the tree-line in summer, and coming lower down in winter. In summer the fur is a light brown; in winter it is almost black. Chamois are gregarious, living in small herds during summer, which join together into herds of 100 or more in winter.
Range: isolated populations occur from France and central Europe to the Balkans and Carpathians. Those in the Pyrenees and Cantabrians are now considered as separate species: *R. pyrenaica.*
Similar Species: most likely to be confused with the Alpine Ibex (*Capra ibex*), which is larger, with larger horns; the Domestic Sheep (*Ovis aries*) and the Domestic Goat (*Capra hircus*) are not as slender as the Chamois, and lack the badger-like face markings.

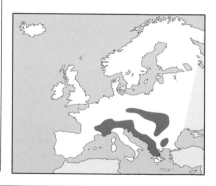

♂ winter

♀ summer

yellowish rump

hoof print

droppings

winter   *summer*

A large deer, greyish brown in winter, reddish brown in summer. The males carry large branching antlers and develop a shaggy mane during the rut, which begins in autumn. The young are heavily spotted. Red Deer vary considerably in size, with some of the largest being found in the forests of eastern Europe, and the smallest on the moorlands of Scotland. Although mostly browsers, they also eat beech mast and acorns in autumn. Largely nocturnal, they often live in close proximity to humans.

Range: widespread over much of Europe, from Iberia to southern Scandinavia; in many areas the Red Deer's range is highly fragmented, particularly in the south.

Similar Species: other deer, particularly the Sika Deer (*C. nippon*) and the Fallow Deer (*C. dama*).

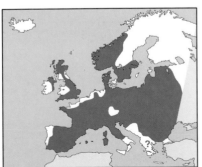

RED DEER	
Type	deer
Habitat	mostly forest, woodland; also more open habitats
Status	formerly more widespread, but not threatened, and increasing in many areas
PHYSICAL DETAILS	
Head & Body	1.7–2.6m
Tail	12–15cm
Weight	70–250kg
Teeth	0.1.3.3 3.1.3.3
Antlers	males only; large, branched
Colour	reddish brown with pale rump
FOOD AND HABITS	
Food	mostly browses on twigs, leaves, shoots
Nest	none
Behaviour	nocturnal and diurnal
Territory	in breeding season male defends harem
Voice	male has belching roar in rut
Hibernation	none
Migration	moves to low ground and sheltered valleys in winter
LIFE CYCLE	
Litters	1a year; early summer
Young	1, occasionally 2; active soon after birth
Maturity	1–2 years
Longevity	up to 20 years

Sika Deer *Cervus nippon*

♂ summer (in velvet)

♀ winter

♂ winter

hoof prints

♀ summer

SIKA DEER	
Type	deer
Habitat	mostly woodland, forest; also parkland
Status	introduced

PHYSICAL DETAILS

Head & Body	1–1.55m
Tail	17–27cm
Weight	17–120kg
Teeth	0.1.3.3
	3.1.3.3
Antlers	males only; branched
Colour	buff with white spots in summer, dark in winter

FOOD AND HABITS

Food	leaves, shoots
Nest	none
Behaviour	diurnal and nocturnal
Voice	male whistles during rut
Hibernation	none
Migration	none

LIFE CYCLE

Litters	1 a year; early summer
Young	usually 1, occasionally 2; active soon after birth
Maturity	about 18 months
Longevity	up to 15 years

The Sika Deer is like a small Red Deer (*C. elaphus*) in shape and proportions, but is spotted in summer and dark in winter (the Red is spotted only as a fawn). The male's antlers are similar to those of the Red, but have fewer branches, and only one forward branch. The two species occasionally interbreed. Sika Deer live in small herds, in woodland, forest, parkland and similar habitats. The fawns are heavily spotted and are active soon after birth.

Range: an Asiatic species that has been widely introduced into many parts of Europe, including Britain and Ireland, and in many places is spreading.

Similar Species: the Red Deer – see above; the Fallow Deer (*C. dama*), which has palmate antlers, and a longer tail with a black centre.

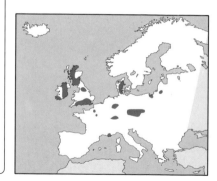

Cervus dama Fallow Deer

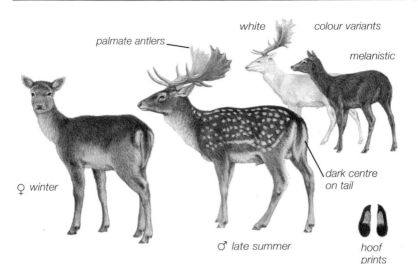

palmate antlers

white — colour variants

melanistic

♀ winter

dark centre on tail

♂ late summer

hoof prints

Mostly seen in parkland, the Fallow Deer is partly domesticated and occurs in several colour varieties. The wild colouring is buff-brown with bold whitish spots on the back, but more uniform colouring, ranging from white to blackish, is common. A distinctive feature of the male is the flattened antlers. The tail is relatively long, with a black line down the centre. The Fallow Deer lives in herds. As well as grazing it also browses, and feeds on acorns in autumn.

Range: probably native to the Mediterranean region, this deer has been introduced into other parts of Europe. It is now widespread in the British Isles, Scandinavia, the Baltic States and elsewhere, living both in the wild and in parkland.

Similar Species: distinguished from all other deer by its rump and tail.

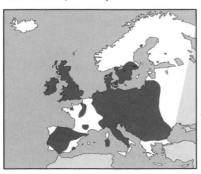

FALLOW DEER

Type	deer
Habitat	parkland, open woodland
Status	not threatened

PHYSICAL DETAILS

Head & Body	1.3–2.3m
Tail	15–20cm
Weight	45–150kg
Teeth	$\frac{0.1.3.3}{3.1.3.3}$
Antlers	males only; palmate
Colour	buff-brown with white spotting; also many variations

FOOD AND HABITS

Food	leaves, shoots, grasses
Nest	none
Behaviour	diurnal and nocturnal
Voice	male has barking grunt in rut
Hibernation	none
Migration	none

LIFE CYCLE

Litters	1 a year; spring
Young	1 or 2; heavily spotted and active within a few days
Maturity	females 2 years, males 3 years
Longevity	up to 20 years

White-tailed Deer *Odocoileus virginianus*

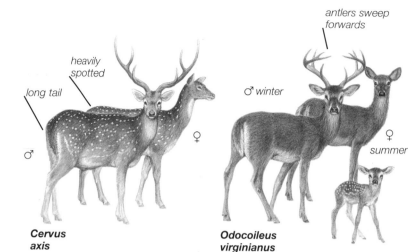

long tail

heavily spotted

♂

♀

Cervus axis

antlers sweep forwards

♂ winter

♀ summer

Odocoileus virginianus

WHITE-TAILED DEER

Type deer
Habitat open woodland
Status introduced

PHYSICAL DETAILS

Head & Body 1.3–2m
Tail 15–33cm
Weight 67.5–135kg
Teeth $\frac{0.1.3.3}{3.1.3.3}$
Antlers males only; branched, bending forwards
Colour reddish brown in summer, grey-brown in winter

FOOD AND HABITS

Food grazes on grasses, browses on leaves, shoots
Nest none
Behaviour nocturnal and diurnal
Voice whistling snort
Hibernation none
Migration none in Europe

LIFE CYCLE

Litters 1 a year; summer
Young usually 1 in 1st year, then twins, occasionally triplets
Maturity females in 2nd year, males in 3rd
Longevity up to 25 years

The White-tailed Deer is midway between the Fallow Deer (*Cervus dama*) and the Red Deer (*C. elaphus*) in size. In summer it is reddish brown, in winter greyish brown. The underside and insides of the ears are white and it has a large white rump patch. The thick tail is brown above, white below. An alarmed deer flicks its tail to expose the white on the tail and the rump. The young are heavily spotted.
Range: introduced from the Americas into Finland, it has spread over much of that and adjacent countries. It has also been introduced in Slovakia, where its range is more restricted.
Similar Species: no other European deer has such a large white rump patch. The Spotted Deer (*C. axis*) is an Asian species, introduced into former Yugoslavia. Both sexes are heavily spotted all year, and the male's antlers are simple.

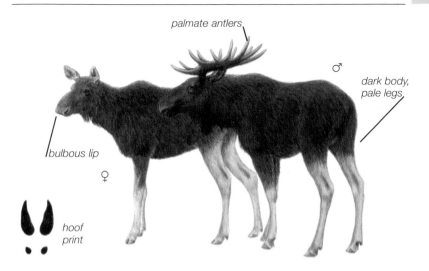

palmate antlers

♂

dark body,
pale legs

bulbous lip

♀

hoof print

A very large deer, standing up to 2.2m at the shoulder. The Elk (known as the Moose in North America) is dark with pale legs. It has a large muzzle and the antlers of the male are usually broad and flattened. Despite its size it can gallop at a speed of over 50km/h. An inhabitant of forests along river valleys and swamps, it frequently wades in water to feed on aquatic vegetation. Its diet also includes shoots of willows, sallows, birch and other trees. It is less gregarious than other deer, and is usually seen singly or in small family groups. The rut is in autumn, when the males have a bugling call, and fight with other males.
Range: widespread in Scandinavia, Russia, and around the Baltic to Poland. Its range is spreading south and westwards to Germany, Czech Republic and Slovakia.
Similar Species: none.

ELK

Type	deer
Habitat	wet woodland, swamp
Status	increasing

PHYSICAL DETAILS

Head & Body	2–3.1m
Tail	c5cm
Weight	up to 800kg
Teeth	0.1.3.3
	3.1.3.3
Antlers	males only; massive, palmate
Colour	brownish black

FOOD AND HABITS

Food	shoots, leaves, grasses, aquatic plants
Nest	none
Behaviour	nocturnal and diurnal
Voice	male has bugling call in rut
Hibernation	none
Migration	none, but wanders extensively

LIFE CYCLE

Litters	1 a year; early summer
Young	1–3, usually 2, rarely 4; active within a few hours
Maturity	female 2 years, male 3 years
Longevity	up to 25 years

Reindeer *Rangifer tarundus*

♀ winter

♂ summer

branched, forward
sweep ot antlers

large hooves

hoof
print

	REINDEER
Type	deer
Habitat	woodland
Status	endangered

PHYSICAL DETAILS

Head & Body	1.7–2.2m
Tail	7–18cm
Weight	120–200kg
Teeth	0.1.3.3
	3.1.3.3
Antlers	both sexes; branched; females smaller
Colour	grey

FOOD AND HABITS

Food	lichens, shoots, grasses, sedges, leaves
Nest	none
Behaviour	diurnal and nocturnal
Voice	normally silent; male snorts during rut
Hibernation	none
Migration	some populations are migratory, moving south during the winter

LIFE CYCLE

Litters	1 a year; spring
Young	normally 1; active within hours of birth
Maturity	in 2nd year
Longevity	c15 years in wild; domesticated variety lives 25–28 years

The only deer to have been successfully domesticated on a large scale. It is also the only deer in which both sexes carry antlers, although the female's are smaller than the male's. The forward branch of the antlers divides again, unlike those of any other deer. The colouring is generally greyish to greyish white. Reindeer are gregarious, often forming large herds. They are confined to Arctic habitats, particularly tundra and woodland.

Range: reduced to scattered populations in Scandinavia; it also occurs eastwards through Russia and has been introduced into Iceland. Domesticated herds are widespread in northern Scandinavia and there is also one in the Cairngorms in Scotland.

Similar Species: domesticated Reindeer, which are smaller, and more variable in colouring.

small, branched antlers

♀ winter

white rump

♂ summer

hoof print

Standing around 75cm at the shoulder, the Roe Deer is the smallest native European deer. It is less gregarious than the Red Deer (*Cervus elaphus*), but may be found in groups of up to about 100 in winter. In summer it is a rich reddish brown, becoming greyer in winter. The young are heavily spotted and the males carry short, spiky, branched antlers. It is usually found in woodland and forests with dense cover, hiding by day and emerging at dusk to feed. Where undisturbed it is also diurnal. The rut is in midsummer. *Range:* most of Europe, including Britain, but absent from most islands. *Similar Species:* Chinese Water Deer (*Hydropotes inermis*) and the Muntjac Deer (*Muntiacus reevesi*), which have been introduced in southern England. The Siberian Roe is considered a separate species and has been introduced into England.

ROE DEER

Type	deer
Habitat	woodland, forests
Status	not threatened

PHYSICAL DETAILS

Head/body	0.9–1.3m
Tail	2.5–3.5cm
Weight	15–35kg
Teeth	$\frac{0.1.3.3}{3.1.3.3}$
Antlers	small, branched
Colour	reddish brown in summer, grey-brown in winter

FOOD AND HABITS

Food	leaves, shoots, grasses
Nest	none, but leaves young hidden in undergrowth
Behaviour	crepuscular and nocturnal, but diurnal where undisturbed
Voice	both sexes have a barking call
Hibernation	none
Migration	none

LIFE CYCLE

Litters	1 a year; early summer
Young	1–3, usually 2; active soon after birth
Maturity	in 2nd year
Longevity	up to 15 years

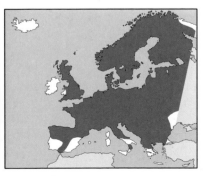

Muntjac Deer *Muntiacus reevesi*

♂ winter

short antlers

♀ summer

hoof print

MUNTJAC DEER	
Type	deer
Habitat	woodlands, gardens, parkland
Status	introduced; spreading
PHYSICAL DETAILS	
Head/body	70–90cm
Tail	up to 12cm
Weight	12–22kg
Teeth	$\frac{0.1.3.3}{3.1.3.3}$
Colour	dark brown
Antlers	very small and simple
FOOD AND HABITS	
Food	leaves, shoots, grasses; also fruit
Nest	none
Behaviour	largely nocturnal and crepuscular
Voice	loud bark, often repeated
Hibernation	none
Migration	none
LIFE CYCLE	
Litters	at 7-month intervals; at almost any time of year
Young	usually 1; active soon after birth
Maturity	in 1st year
Longevity	12–14 years

A very small deer, standing less than 50cm at the shoulder. It is rather dark, and the short, fairly broad tail conceals the white rump, which is only exposed when it is fleeing. The male's antlers are extremely small, and grow from prominent brows; the male also has small tusks. The young are heavily spotted. Muntjac Deer are also known as Barking Deer, and because of their skulking, secretive habits they are often only detected by the distinctive loud bark. They are generally solitary or live in pairs, and are territorial.

Range: an Asiatic species introduced into England, it is now widespread and locally abundant in many southern parts of the country.

Similar Species: the Chinese Water Deer (*Hydropotes inermis*) is lighter in colouring and lacks antlers; the Roe Deer (*Capreolus capreolus*) is larger.

lacks white rump

♀

fawn

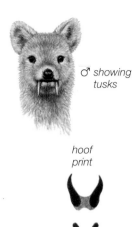

♂ showing tusks

hoof print

This is the only deer found in Europe that lacks antlers in both sexes. A small deer, it stands less than 60cm at the shoulder. The colouring is sandy brown, without an obvious rump pattern. The ears are relatively large and the male has prominent tusks (up to 8cm long). Chinese Water Deer are generally nocturnal, living in woodland, marshes and more open areas, but their presence is often difficult to detect. Although they are prolific they suffer heavy mortality.

Range: originally from Asia, it has, since the 1940s, become established in central and eastern England.

Similar Species: the Muntjac Deer (*Muntiacus reevesi*) is smaller and always darker. The Roe Deer (*Capreolus capreolus*) is larger. In summer it is more rufous, and in winter greyer, with a conspicuous white rump.

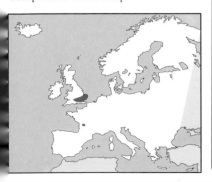

CHINESE WATER DEER	
Type	deer
Habitat	marshes, woodlands, parkland
Status	introduced
PHYSICAL DETAILS	
Head/body	0.75–1.05m
Tail	5–8cm
Weight	12–22kg
Teeth	0.1.3.3
	3.1.3.3
Colour	sandy brown
FOOD AND HABITS	
Food	shoots, leaves, grasses
Nest	none
Behaviour	largely nocturnal and crepuscular
Voice	male has whistling call during rut; screams like a hare when alarmed
Hibernation	none
Migration	none
LIFE CYCLE	
Litters	1 a year; late spring–early summer
Young	1–6, usually 2–4
Maturity	in 1st year
Longevity	no data

Fin Whale *Balaenoptera physalis*

fin more prominent
than *B. musculus*

ridge

ridge

FIN WHALE

Type	whale
Habitat	marine
Status	endangered

PHYSICAL DETAILS

Length	up to 26.8m
Weight	up to 69.5 tonnes
Teeth	none; replaced by baleen plates
Colour	dark grey above, whitish below

FOOD AND HABITS

Food	zooplankton, small fish
Nest	none
Behaviour	dives for 5–15 mins
Voice	repetitive low frequency sounds, at around 20kHz
Hibernation	none
Migration	moves to tropical waters during the winter

LIFE CYCLE

Litters	1 every other year; winter
Young	1; active from birth
Maturity	6–7 years
Longevity	c100 years

This is one of the largest whales, and was once abundant in European waters. Like all rorquals it is slender and has a small dorsal fin set well back on the body. The Fin Whale is unusual in having asymmetrical colouring: the right-hand side of the lower jaw is pale, whereas the left is dark. When surfacing it normally breaks the water with the head first, gives a single blow (4–6m high), then slowly rolls forward and down, exposing the dorsal fin, before diving. Fin Whales often travel in pods of 6–15.

Range: found in all European seas and oceans, but populations are severely depleted. It is occasionally seen in the Mediterranean, but is most frequently observed off the Hebrides, around Iceland, and east to Norway.

Similar Species: other rorquals, none of which have the asymmetrical markings.

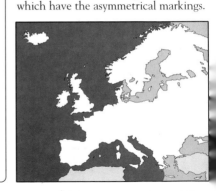

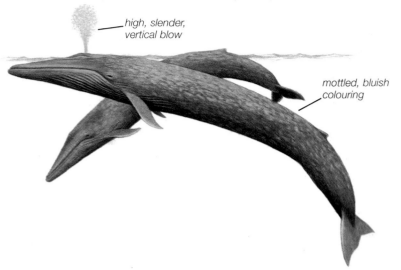

high, slender,
vertical blow

mottled, bluish
colouring

The Blue Whale is the largest animal that has ever lived. Like other rorquals it is streamlined and has grooves on its throat. Its dorsal fin is proportionally smaller than in other rorquals, and it surfaces almost horizontally so that the blowhole and back appear to break water almost simultaneously; the single blow is 6–12m high. When it dives the tail flukes are usually exposed. Blue Whales live in family groups of 3 or 4, which may join with others at good feeding grounds.

Range: once widespread in all European marine waters, Blue Whales have, since the turn of the present century, been eliminated from most areas, and are now rare. They are most likely to be seen in Atlantic waters.

Similar Species: the Fin Whale (*B. physalis*) rarely shows its flukes as it dives, and has a larger dorsal fin.

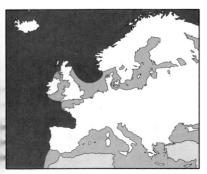

BLUE WHALE

Type	whale
Habitat	marine
Status	endangered

PHYSICAL DETAILS

Length	up to 31m
Weight	up to 178 tonnes
Teeth	none; replaced by baleen plates
Colour	blue-grey

FOOD AND HABITS

Food	krill, other zooplankton
Nest	none
Behaviour	normally up to 20 dives of about 20 secs, followed by a longer dive of up to 30 mins
Voice	pulses of 21–31kHz when feeding; also low frequency moans
Hibernation	none
Migration	moves to warmer waters in winter

LIFE CYCLE

Litters	1 every 3 years; winter
Young	1; active from birth, and feeding
Maturity	7–10 years
Longevity	c100 years

Sei Whale *Balaenoptera borealis*

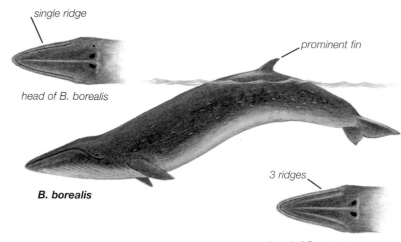

single ridge

head of B. borealis

prominent fin

B. borealis

3 ridges

head of B. edenii

SEI WHALE

Type	whale
Habitat	marine
Status	endangered

PHYSICAL DETAILS

Length	up to 20m
Weight	up to 29 tonnes
Teeth	none; replaced by baleen plates
Colour	blue-grey, paler on throat

FOOD AND HABITS

Food	krill, cephalopods, capelin, other small fish
Nest	none
Behaviour	2 or 3 blows; dives for 5–6 mins
Voice	includes clicks at 3kHz
Hibernation	none
Migration	migrates to tropical waters in winter

LIFE CYCLE

Litters	1 every other year; winter
Young	1; active from birth
Maturity	probably c10 years
Longevity	c70 years

In shape, colouring and proportions the Sei Whale is similar to the Blue Whale (*B. musculus*). However, even when fully grown it is much smaller. It feeds close to the surface, and breaks the water almost horizontally, exposing the head, back and dorsal fin almost simultaneously. The blow is up to 3m. Stranded Sei Whales can be distinguished by the number of throat pleats: they have an average of 52, whereas Blue and Fin Whales always have more than 55. Sei Whales usually travel in small family groups, sometimes congregating on the feeding grounds. *Range:* formerly abundant in North Atlantic waters, it is now very rare. *Similar species:* Bryde's Whale (*B. edenii*) is a tropical species which can occur as a vagrant in European waters. It cannot reliably be distinguished except at close quarters.

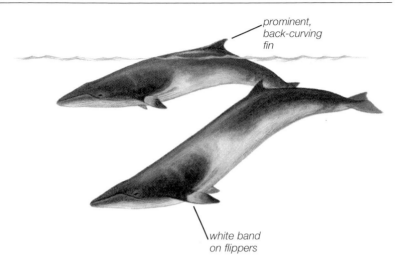

prominent,
back-curving
fin

white band
on flippers

Also known as the Little Piked Whale or Lesser Rorqual, the Minke Whale is the smallest of the rorquals. It is slightly less streamlined than the other species, with a more pointed upper jaw. Its most distinctive feature is the white patch on the upper surface of the flipper, which varies in size. The blow is less visible than in some other whales. Minke usually travel singly or in small family groups, feeding largely on fish. They are mostly seen between June and October, which is also when most strandings occur.

Range: widespread in the North Atlantic, and more common in estuaries and coastal waters than other rorquals. It is most abundant in Scottish, Norwegian and Icelandic waters.

Similar Species: not likely to be confused with other species at close quarters; all other rorquals are larger.

MINKE WHALE
Type	whale
Habitat	marine
Status	very depleted, but probably not endangered

PHYSICAL DETAILS
Length	up to 9.4m
Weight	up to 9 tonnes
Teeth	none; replaced by baleen plates
Colour	dark grey above, paler below, white patch on flipper

FOOD AND HABITS
Food	krill, herrings, sand eels, capelin, other fish
Nest	none
Behaviour	5–8 blows; dives for up to 30 mins
Voice	wide range, including clicks at 4–8kHz, and other calls at 100–200kHz
Hibernation	none
Migration	moves into Arctic waters in summer

LIFE CYCLE
Litters	1, possibly every 18 months; at almost any time of year
Young	1; active from birth
Maturity	c6 years
Longevity	c50 years

Humpback Whale *Megaptera novaeangliae*

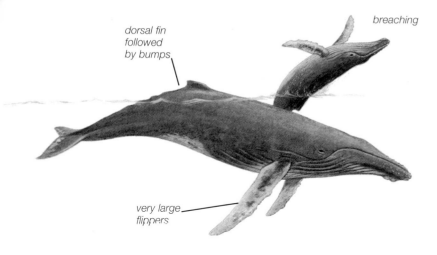

dorsal fin
followed
by bumps

breaching

very large
flippers

HUMPBACK WHALE

Type	whale
Habitat	marine
Status	endangered

PHYSICAL DETAILS

Length	up to 19m
Weight	up to 48 tonnes
Teeth	none; replaced by baleen plates
Colour	grey above, whitish below, with white on flippers

FOOD AND HABITS

Food	krill, herring, capelin
Nest	none
Behaviour	blows several times on surface for 2–3 mins, then dives for 3–28 mins
Voice	elaborate range of songs, up to 15 mins each
Hibernation	none
Migration	moves from Arctic in winter to breed in warm tropical waters

LIFE CYCLE

Litters	1 every other year; winter
Young	1; active from birth
Maturity	c10 years
Longevity	c50 years

One of the most distinctive of all whales, the Humpback frequently breaches, often becoming clearly visible. Unlike the rorquals it is not particularly streamlined, and it nearly always exposes the large tail as it dives; like the rorquals the dorsal fin is rather small and set well back. Its most distinctive feature is the huge flippers, up to 5m long, with a heavily scalloped edge. The blow is short and globular. Humpbacks perform a wide range of apparently playful activities such as slapping the water with their flippers and back somersaults. They normally travel in pods of 3 or 4.

Range: recorded in most European waters, but now extremely rare. However, in the western Atlantic it may be increasing.

Similar Species: all other whales have much smaller flippers.

low 'bushy' blow

no dorsal fin

calloused bonnet

The right whales are so-called because they were the right ones to kill: large, slow moving, and floating when dead. They are massive, with a huge head, and no dorsal fin. Although almost entirely black, they sometimes have small amounts of white on the underside, and whitish callosities on the head. The blowholes are widely separated, producing a 'V' shaped blow, about 5m high. While breathing, much of the top of the head and back is exposed above water, and as they dive the tail shows clearly.

Range: very rare, and most likely to be seen off northern Spain and the Bay of Biscay, north to Iceland.

Similar Species: the Bowhead Whale (*B. mysticetus*), which has a proportionally larger head, lacks callosities, and usually has white on its lower jaw.

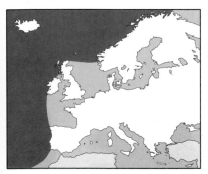

BLACK RIGHT WHALE

Type	whale
Habitat	marine
Status	endangered

PHYSICAL DETAILS

Length	up to 18m
Weight	up to 96 tonnes
Teeth	none; replaced by baleen plates
Colour	black, some white markings

FOOD AND HABITS

Food	krill, other zooplankton
Nest	none
Behaviour	cruises at the surface for about 5–10 mins, then dives for 10–20 mins
Voice	a wide range of sounds, 160–2100Hz
Hibernation	none
Migration	moves to warmer waters in winter

LIFE CYCLE

Litters	1 every 3 years; winter
Young	1; active from birth
Maturity	no data
Longevity	no data

Bowhead Whale *Balaena mysticetus*

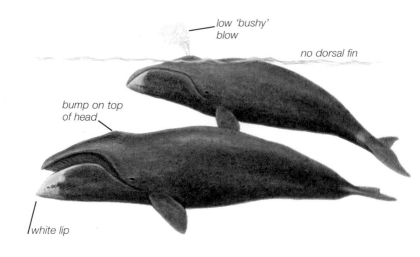

low 'bushy' blow

no dorsal fin

bump on top of head

white lip

BOWHEAD
Type	whale
Habitat	marine
Status	endangered

PHYSICAL DETAILS
Length	up to 20m
Weight	up to 110 tonnes
Teeth	none; replaced by baleen plates
Colour	black, often with white on chin

FOOD AND HABITS
Food	krill, zooplankton
Nest	none
Behaviour	usually breathes for 3 mins, then dives for up to 20 mins
Voice	probably similar to Black Right Whale
Hibernation	none
Migration	moves south during winter; follows retreat of ice northwards in summer

LIFE CYCLE
Litters	1 every other year; midwinter
Young	1, occasionally 2; active from birth
Maturity	10 years
Longevity	possibly 1–2 centuries

Also known as the Greenland Right Whale, the Bowhead is very similar in general appearance to the Black Right Whale (*B. glacialis*). Like that species it is a largely coastal whale, found almost exclusively in Arctic waters. Eskimos have claimed that it can break through ice up to 1m thick to breathe. It is one of the rarest mammals in the world.
Range: in European waters the Bowhead probably once occurred in northern Scandinavia east to Spitzbergen, and it may have occurred around Iceland. However, the systematic collection of field sightings of living whales is only a relatively recent practice, and remnant populations may be discovered by naturalists visiting Arctic waters.
Similar Species: the Black Right Whale, which lacks white on its lower jaw and has callosities on its head.

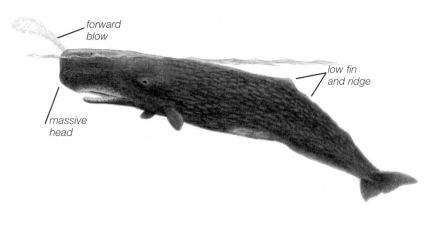

forward blow

low fin and ridge

massive head

The largest of the toothed whales, the Sperm Whale is recognized by its massive head, and relatively small jaws with peg-like teeth on the lower jaw only. Males are much larger than females. The blow is directed forwards and to the left, about 3–5m; the first blow after a dive can be heard for a kilometre or more. Sperm Whales have a complex social structure. When one is injured or a female is giving birth, others will come to help. A whole pod will sometimes die as a result of one whale becoming stranded.

Range: occurs widely in warmer tropical waters; the males migrate north in summer and are often found in European waters, north to the Arctic; it is still regularly recorded in the Mediterranean.

Similar Species: not likely to be confused with any other whale.

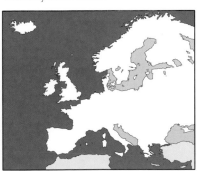

	SPERM WHALE
Type	whale
Habitat	marine
Status	depleted
	PHYSICAL DETAILS
Length	up to 20m, usually 11–15m
Weight	up to 38 tonnes
Teeth	$\dfrac{0}{18\text{–}29}$
Colour	greyish
	FOOD AND HABITS
Food	mostly squid and other cephalopods
Nest	none
Behaviour	breathes on surface for c10 mins, then dives for up to 50 mins
Voice	echolocating clicks
Hibernation	none
Migration	moves to warm tropical waters in winter
	LIFE CYCLE
Litters	1 every 4 years; winter
Young	1, occasionally 2; active from birth
Maturity	females c10 years; males 25 years
Longevity	up to 70 years

Pygmy Sperm Whale *Kogia breviceps*

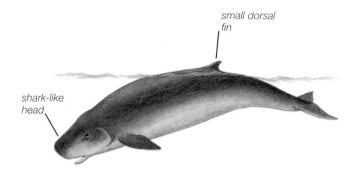

small dorsal fin

shark-like head

	PYGMY SPERM WHALE
Type	whale
Habitat	marine
Status	vagrant to European waters

	PHYSICAL DETAILS
Length	up to 3.4m
Weight	up to 400kg
Teeth	0 / 12–16
Colour	grey with a pinkish tinge

	FOOD AND HABITS
Food	squid, fish, crustaceans
Nest	none
Behaviour	rests at surface; dives slowly
Voice	clicks, possibly used for echolocation
Hibernation	none
Migration	unknown

	LIFE CYCLE
Litters	probably 1 every other year; winter
Young	probably 1; active from birth
Maturity	no data
Longevity	no data

Although it is a mostly tropical species, the Pygmy Sperm Whale occasionally becomes stranded on Atlantic coasts. Like the Sperm Whale (*Physeter catodon*) it has a row of peg-like teeth, on the lower jaw only. It feeds on squid, fish, and some crustaceans. It surfaces slowly and rarely breaches. If surprised on the surface it defecates while diving, leaving a rust-coloured stain on the water.

Range: strandings occur mostly on the French coastline, but have also been recorded in the Netherlands, Portugal and Ireland.

Similar Species: the Dwarf Sperm Whale (*K. simus*), is very similar but smaller (less than 2.7m), with a larger dorsal fin, positioned further forward. It may occur in waters around south-west Europe. Dolphins are faster-swimming and have a larger dorsal fin.

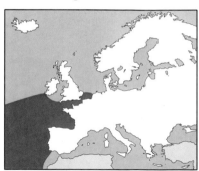

bulbous forehead

small, curving fin

short beak

A large, toothed whale, distinctive for its combination of a rounded head ('melon'), a beak and a relatively small dorsal fin. Normally very gregarious, it lives in family groups of up to 10 or more, comprising a male with several females and young. It is attracted to boats, and often approaches them closely, making it easy prey. Bottle-nosed Whales often 'lobtail', and slap their tail very noisily on the water's surface, and young ones sometimes leap out of the water. Hunting has reduced their numbers greatly since the time when they could apparently be observed across the entire Atlantic Ocean.

Range: confined to the northern Atlantic, where despite hunting it remains one of the more frequently observed species.

Similar Species: none within range.

BOTTLE-NOSED WHALE	
Type	whale
Habitat	marine
Status	depleted, but not endangered
PHYSICAL DETAILS	
Length	up to 10m
Weight	up to 5.4 tonnes
Teeth	$\frac{?0}{2}$
Colour	grey-brown to blackish
FOOD AND HABITS	
Food	mostly squid; also herring, starfish
Nest	none
Behaviour	breathes for several mins, then dives for up to 30 mins
Voice	wide range of clicks and whistles
Hibernation	none
Migration	moves south from colder waters in winter
LIFE CYCLE	
Litters	1 a year; spring
Young	1; active from birth
Maturity	9–12 years
Longevity	30–40 years

Cuvier's Whale *Ziphius cavirostris*

head
often
white

heavily scarred

CUVIER'S WHALE

Type whale
Habitat marine
Status little known, but probably not threatened

PHYSICAL DETAILS

Length up to 7m
Weight up to 4.5 tonnes
Teeth females none
males $\frac{0}{2}$
Colour variable, usually grey

FOOD AND HABITS

Food squid, starfish, crabs and fish
Nest none
Behaviour blows at 20 sec intervals
Voice unknown
Hibernation none
Migration moves into northern waters in late summer

LIFE CYCLE

Litters 1 a year; at any time of year
Young probably 1; active from birth
Maturity no data
Longevity c60 years

Cuvier's or the Goosebeak Whale is a medium-sized whale that is rarely seen, except when stranded. It has the tapering shape of a beaked whale, but its colouring is variable, ranging from uniform grey to white above and grey or black below. Males have two tusks in the lower jaw. Cuvier's Whales are often scarred with white patches and other marks; males have parallel scars on the back produced by the teeth of other males. These whales surface with the dome of the head showing, blow with a puff of spray, and then roll forward, exposing the tail as they dive. They live in pods of up to 15.
Range: strandings have been recorded off the western coasts of the British Isles, but it is more commonly found in warmer waters off France and Spain, in the Atlantic and the Mediterranean.
Similar Species: other beaked whales.

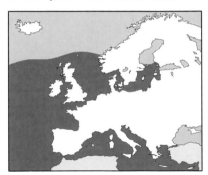

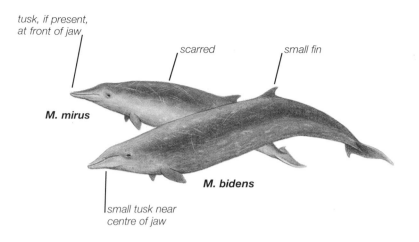

tusk, if present, at front of jaw

scarred

small fin

M. mirus

M. bidens

small tusk near centre of jaw

The only beaked whale that is commonly seen in colder Arctic waters, Sowerby's has the most northerly range of the group. When surfacing it raises its head and beak above the water, breathes, then slowly curves over, exposing the dorsal fin but not the tail. Only the male normally has teeth, one on each lower jaw, set well back. Males and females live in pairs.

Range: occurs in the North Atlantic, the North Sea and Baltic, around the British Isles, and north to Iceland.
Similar Species: True's Beaked Whale (M. *mirus*), and Gervais' Beaked Whale (M. *europaeus*) have been recorded in European waters, mostly as strandings; Gray's Beaked Whale (M. *grayi*), and Blainville's Beaked Whale (M. *densirostris*) may also occur, particularly off Spain and Portugal.

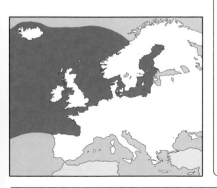

SOWERBY'S BEAKED WHALE	
Type	whale
Habitat	marine
Status	little known, but probably not threatened

PHYSICAL DETAILS	
Length	c5m
Weight	up to 1.3 tonnes
Teeth	females none males $\frac{0}{1}$
Colour	dark grey above, pale below; often white on jaw

FOOD AND HABITS	
Food	squid, small fish
Nest	none
Behaviour	unknown
Voice	unknown
Hibernation	none
Migration	probably moves north in summer to edge of Arctic ice

LIFE CYCLE	
Litters	probably 1 a year; winter
Young	probably 1; active from birth
Maturity	no data
Longevity	no data

White Whale *Delphinapterus leucas*

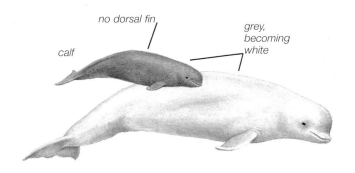

no dorsal fin

calf

grey, becoming white

WHITE WHALE

Type	whale
Habitat	marine
Status	vagrant to most northern European waters

PHYSICAL DETAILS

Length	up to 4.6m
Weight	up to 1 tonne
Teeth	up to $\frac{11}{8 \text{ or } 9}$
Colour	white when adult

FOOD AND HABITS

Food	fish, crustaceans
Nest	none
Behaviour	breathes once or twice a min, then dives for up to 15 mins
Voice	sonar; uses clicks to navigate
Hibernation	none
Migration	migrates to edge of pack ice in summer

LIFE CYCLE

Litters	1 every 2–3 years; winter
Young	1; active from birth
Maturity	5–8 years
Longevity	50+ years

The adult White Whale or Beluga is unmistakable, being a pure white in colour. Newborn whales are pinkish brown. They gradually turn dark grey, before becoming white at maturity. The head is rounded and there is no dorsal fin. White Whales are gregarious, living in groups of up to 10, and sometimes gathering in herds of several thousand. They are mainly marine, but occasionally enter rivers and estuaries. Feeding mostly along the sea bed, they eat capelin, cod, char and sand eels, as well as crustaceans.

Range: confined to the colder, Arctic waters; some populations are sedentary, others migrate, occasionally straying into European waters.

Similar Species: most likely to be confused with the Narwhal (*Monodon monoceros*), which is usually greyer, and often has a long tusk.

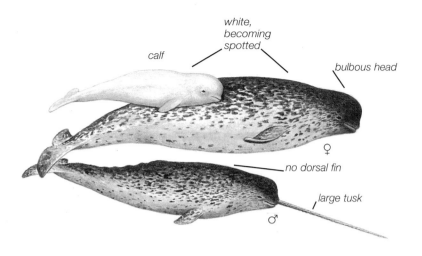

calf

white, becoming spotted

bulbous head

♀

no dorsal fin

large tusk

♂

The Narwhal is slightly larger than the White Whale or Beluga (*Delphinapterus leucas*). It is heavily dappled with dark grey above, and the males carry a single, long tusk (up to 2m or more). The tusk is an extraordinary development of the left tooth; occasionally a right-hand tusk develops and females occasionally have one or two small tusks. Narwhals live in groups of 6–10, but during migration may form much larger herds.

Range: it shares the range of the Beluga and is confined to colder Arctic waters, but occasional vagrants occur in northern European waters, as far south as the North Sea.

Similar Species: most likely to be confused with the White Whale, which is generally paler (adults are pure white) and never has a tusk.

NARWHAL

Type	whale
Habitat	marine
Status	vagrant to northern European waters

PHYSICAL DETAILS

Length	c5m
Weight	up to 1.8 tonnes
Teeth	females none; males $\frac{1}{0}$ tusk
Colour	pale grey with dark dappling

FOOD AND HABITS

Food	squid, fish (particularly flatfish), crabs, other crustaceans
Nest	none
Behaviour	breathes every 30–50 secs
Voice	very vocal; clicks, whistles, growls
Hibernation	none
Migration	moves south during winter

LIFE CYCLE

Litters	1 every 3 years; winter
Young	1; active from birth
Maturity	6–10 years
Longevity	40–50 years

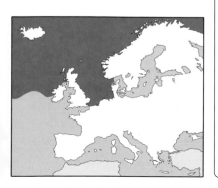

Long-finned Pilot Whale _Globicephala melaena_

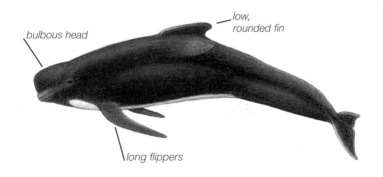

bulbous head

low, rounded fin

long flippers

LONG-FINNED PILOT WHALE

Type	whale
Habitat	marine
Status	seriously depleted

PHYSICAL DETAILS

Length	up to 8.5m
Weight	up to 3.8 tonnes
Teeth	$\frac{20-22}{7-12}$
Colour	black with white on throat and belly

FOOD AND HABITS

Food	squid, fish
Nest	none
Behaviour	breathes once every 2–3 mins, then dives for 5–10 mins
Voice	wide range of clicks, squeaks, whistles, chirps and other sounds
Hibernation	none
Migration	moves south in winter

LIFE CYCLE

Litters	1 every 2–3 years; at any time of year
Young	1; active from birth
Maturity	6–12 years
Longevity	40–60 years

A medium-sized whale with a rounded head. It is most easily identified by the large, curved dorsal fin, set well forward. The body is almost entirely black or dark grey but with a slightly paler patch behind the fin, and white on the underside, particularly along the centre of the belly. Long-finned Pilot Whales are highly gregarious, travelling in pods of up to 200, occasionally many more. This, and the fact that they try to help the injured, makes them easy prey for hunters.

Range: widespread in the North Atlantic, the North Sea and also the Mediterranean, but populations have collapsed.

Similar Species: the Short-Finned Pilot Whale (_Globiocephalus macrorhynchus_) is a tropical species that has been recorded in European waters. It has proportionally smaller flippers.

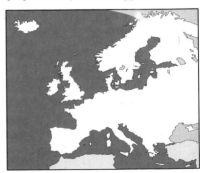

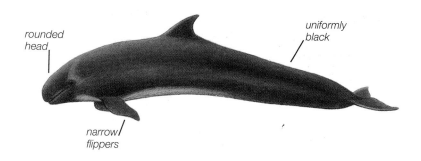

rounded head

uniformly black

narrow flippers

Only superficially similar to the Killer Whale (*Orcinus orca*), the False Killer Whale is more likely to be confused with the pilot whales. It is gregarious, living in groups of 4–6, and is one of the largest whales to ride the bow waves of ships. When it surfaces, its head, dorsal fin and a large part of its back are visible. It is regularly stranded, when the teeth are distinctive, being up to 2.5cm in diameter and round in cross-section (the Killer Whale's are oval). It eats fish up to the size of bonito and tuna, as well as squid. *Range:* it has been recorded in the eastern North Atlantic, North Sea and the Mediterranean, where it is rare. *Similar Species:* the Killer Whale and the Pilot Whale – see above. The Pygmy Killer Whale (*Feresa attenuata*) is smaller and has a white patch on the lower lip.

FALSE KILLER WHALE	
Type	whale
Habitat	marine
Status	not threatened

PHYSICAL DETAILS	
Length	up to 5.4m
Weight	2.2 tonnes
Teeth	7–10 / 9–12
Colour	dark grey or black

FOOD AND HABITS	
Food	squid, fish
Nest	none
Behaviour	breathes every 15–20 secs, then dives
Voice	unknown
Hibernation	none
Migration	unknown

LIFE CYCLE	
Litters	1 every 2–3 years; at any time of year
Young	1; active from birth
Maturity	8–12 years
Longevity	40–60 years

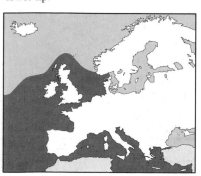

Killer Whale *Orcinus orca*

white patch

large dorsal fin

large, rounded flippers

♂

♀

KILLER WHALE

Type	whale
Habitat	marine
Status	not threatened

PHYSICAL DETAILS

Length	up to 9.75m
Weight	up to 7.2 tonnes
Teeth	10–13
	10–13
Colour	black and white

FOOD AND HABITS

Food	mammals, birds, squid
Nest	none
Behaviour	5 or 6 short dives, followed by a dive of 1–4 mins
Voice	uses sonar to navigate
Hibernation	none
Migration	no regular patterns noted

LIFE CYCLE

Litters	1 every 2–3 years; at almost any time of year
Young	1; active from birth
Maturity	5–6 years
Longevity	50–80 years

The Killer Whale or Orca is a medium-sized cetacean, distinctive for its black and white colouring and a very tall (up to 2m), shark-like, triangular dorsal fin. Occurring in all oceans, it is exclusively marine and often travels in pods of 5–20. It is carnivorous, with long, sharp teeth (up to 12cm). Often hunting in packs, it preys on other cetaceans, including young rorquals and other great whales, as well as seals, sea birds, squid and fish.

Range: widespread in European waters, occurring in the Atlantic Ocean, the North and Baltic Seas and the Mediterranean Ocean. It is most abundant in the north of its range.

Similar Species: the superficially similar False Killer Whale (*Pseudorca crassidens*), is difficult to distinguish at a distance. At close range it can be seen to lack the white patches.

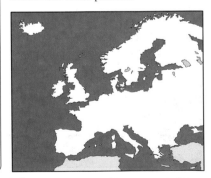

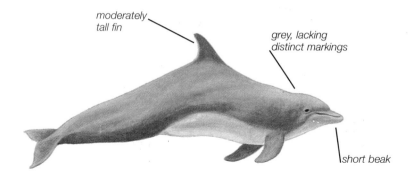

moderately tall fin

grey, lacking distinct markings

short beak

The most familiar dolphin, with a distinctive, prominent beak. The colouring is bluish grey above, paler below. Bottle-nosed Dolphins usually occur in small groups in European waters. They often ride the bow waves of boats. Although primarily marine, these dolphins are found in lagoons, bays, and sometimes rivers. They are regularly stranded. Feeding on fish, they sometimes follow fishing boats, catching disturbed fish.

Range: occurs most commonly in the Atlantic and Mediterranean, but also in all other European seas. Although once very abundant in the Black Sea, it has been heavily hunted.

Similar Species: other dolphins are all more contrastingly marked. The Common Porpoise (*Phocoena phocoena*) is smaller, lacks a beak and has only a small fin.

BOTTLE-NOSED DOLPHIN

Type	dolphin
Habitat	marine, coastal
Status	depleted

PHYSICAL DETAILS

Length	up to 4m
Weight	usually up to 200kg (rarely 650kg)
Teeth	$\frac{18-26}{18-26}$
Colour	blue-grey above, paler below

FOOD AND HABITS

Food	mostly fish; also crustaceans
Nest	none
Behaviour	breaks the surface 2–3 times a min when breathing; dives for up to 10 mins
Voice	wide range of squeaks and chirps
Hibernation	none
Migration	moves to warmer waters in winter

LIFE CYCLE

Litters	1 a year; summer
Young	1; active from birth
Maturity	c6 years
Longevity	up to 30 years

Risso's Dolphin *Grampus griseus*

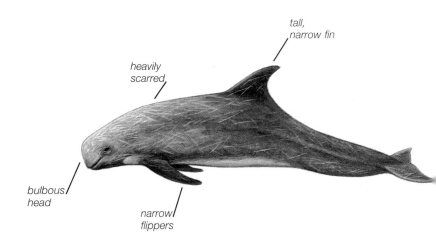

tall, narrow fin

heavily scarred

bulbous head

narrow flippers

RISSO'S DOLPHIN
Type	whale
Habitat	marine
Status	not threatened

PHYSICAL DETAILS
Length	up to 4m
Weight	up to 680kg
Teeth	$\frac{0}{2-7}$
Colour	grey

FOOD AND HABITS
Food	squid, fish
Nest	none
Behaviour	blows every 20–30 secs for 3–4 mins, then dives
Voice	unknown
Hibernation	none
Migration	unknown

LIFE CYCLE
Litters	1 a year; winter
Young	1; active from birth
Maturity	c8 years
Longevity	25–90 years

Risso's Dolphin or the Grampus is superficially similar to the pilot whales, but is greyer with shorter flippers, and a taller fin. It commonly lives in groups of 25 or more, occasionally several hundred, often in association with other cetaceans, particularly pilot whales. Spending most of its time in deeper waters, it feeds principally on squid, as well as fish. It is more frequently stranded than most other species, when it is easily identified by the extensive scarring on its body.
Range: widely distributed in European waters, including the Mediterranean, and possibly the Black Sea.
Similar Species: the pilot whales and the False Killer Whale (*Pseudorca crassidens*), which have darker colouring; the Bottle-nosed Dolphin (*Tursiops truncatus*), which has a beak and a shorter dorsal fin.

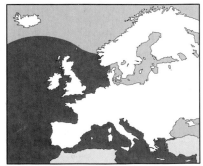

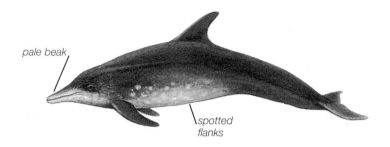

pale beak

spotted
flanks

A small, little-known dolphin that has been recorded in European waters only as a few isolated strandings. It is streamlined with a tapering beak and is distinctively coloured: dark grey above, white below, with whitish or pinkish scarring. Rough-toothed Dolphins are gregarious, often travelling in schools of up to 50, and they ride the bow waves of ships. Stranded specimens are identified by examining the teeth, which have fine vertical ridges and furrows, giving them a matt finish.
Range: a tropical Atlantic species, only occasionally straying into European waters, mostly in the south-west, including the Mediterranean.
Similar Species: the Striped (*Stenella coeruleoalba*) and Bottle-nosed (*Tursiops truncatus*) Dolphins, both of which have the beak more clearly separated from the head, and lack prominent spotting.

ROUGH-TOOTHED DOLPHIN

Type	whale
Habitat	marine
Status	vagrant to European waters

PHYSICAL DETAILS

Length	up to 2.75m
Weight	c160kg
Teeth	$\frac{20-27}{20-27}$
Colour	grey above, white below, with whitish or pinkish scarring

FOOD AND HABITS

Food	cephalopods, fish
Nest	none
Behaviour	breathes every 7–10 secs, then dives
Voice	range of clicks for echolocating
Hibernation	none
Migration	unknown

LIFE CYCLE

Litters	1 a year; summer
Young	1; active from birth
Maturity	10–14 years
Longevity	no data

Common Dolphin *Delphinus delphus*

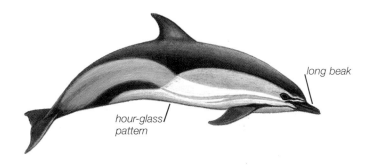

long beak

hour-glass pattern

COMMON DOLPHIN
Type whale
Habitat marine
Status depleted

PHYSICAL DETAILS
Length up to 2.6m
Weight up to 136kg
Teeth $\dfrac{40-57}{40-57}$
Colour variable patterning of black, yellowish, grey and white, usually with black eye patches

FOOD AND HABITS
Food squid, fish
Nest none
Behaviour breathes several times a min, then dives, usually for less than 5 mins
Voice echolocation clicks; 100–159kHz
Hibernation none
Migration none recorded, but moves extensively

LIFE CYCLE
Litters 1 every 2–3 years; summer
Young usually 1; active from birth
Maturity c6 years
Longevity c30 years

A streamlined dolphin, with a prominent beak. Its colouring is distinctive: dark grey above, white below, with variable markings of paler grey and buff-yellow. The flippers are blackish and there is usually a dark eye patch. It is very gregarious, travelling in large schools, often riding bow waves and leaping out of the water. It rarely dives for more than a few minutes, preferring to swim close to the surface. Schools of up to 250,000 were once reported, but extensive hunting has caused considerable depletion. It is still hunted in some places.
Range: widespread in all European seas, north to Iceland and Norway and east to the Black Sea.
Similar Species: most likely to be confused with other dolphins, but none have the distinctive colouring and patterning and few are as abundant.

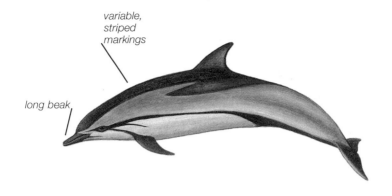

variable,
striped
markings

long beak

The Striped or Euphrosyne Dolphin is closely related to several other species, notably the Spinner Dolphin (*S. longirostris*) and Spotted Dolphin (*S. plagiodon*), from which it can be very difficult to distinguish. It often rides the bow wave of boats, when the distinctive striped pattern can often be seen. The colouring varies from shades of grey to brownish above and white below, with a pattern reminiscent of the Common Dolphin (*Delphinus delphus*), but without yellowish markings.

Range: widespread in most European waters, including the Mediterranean; sometimes stranded, rarely observed.

Similar Species: the Spinner Dolphin is a tropical species, also with a long beak, and is noted for its acrobatic breaching. It may occur in southern Spanish and Portuguese waters.

STRIPED DOLPHIN	
Type	whale
Habitat	marine
Status	rarely recorded
PHYSICAL DETAILS	
Length	up to 3m
Weight	up to 130kg
Teeth	43–49 / 43–49
Colour	grey or buffy grey above, white below
FOOD AND HABITS	
Food	small fish
Nest	none
Behaviour	unknown
Voice	unknown
Hibernation	none
Migration	moves to warmer waters in winter
LIFE CYCLE	
Litters	1 every 3 years; autumn
Young	probably 1; active from birth
Maturity	5–9 years
Longevity	c30 years

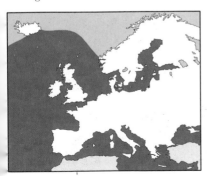

White-sided Dolphin *Lagenorhynchus acutus*

dark above,
pale below

pale patch

WHITE-SIDED DOLPHIN
Type whale
Habitat marine
Status not threatened

PHYSICAL DETAILS
Length up to 3m
Weight up to 250kg
Teeth 30–40
30–40
Colour grey, yellowish and white

FOOD AND HABITS
Food squid, fish, particularly herring
Nest none
Behaviour breathes several times a min
Voice probably makes echolocating clicks
Hibernation none
Migration may move south during winter

LIFE CYCLE
Litters 1 a year; spring
Young probably 1; active from birth
Maturity 5–7 years
Longevity no data

Despite its name, the best way of distinguishing this species from the related White-beaked Dolphin (*L. albirostris*) is by the fact that it has very little white on its sides. It is dark grey above, lighter grey on the sides, with a white belly and a dirty yellow patch on the flanks behind the dorsal fin. An acrobatic species, it is often seen leaping out of the water. It lives in groups of up to 50, which often form schools of 1000 or more.
Range: confined to northern European waters, from the Arctic Ocean to the North Sea and (rarely) on both sides of the English Channel. In the British Isles it is most abundant around Orkney and Shetland.
Similar Species: the White-beaked Dolphin, which has more white on its sides, a white upper jaw and a blunter dorsal fin.

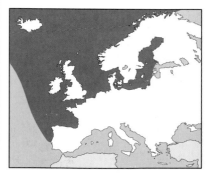

large fin

pale beak

The White-beaked Dolphin is one of the most northerly dolphins. It is similar to the White-sided Dolphin (*L. acutus*), with a short beak, but has more white on its sides, and both its upper and lower jaws are white. It is gregarious, forming schools of up to 1500, but living in groups of 6–30 within the schools. In the northern parts of its range it is the only dolphin likely to be encountered, but further south it overlaps with several others. *Range:* most common in Arctic waters, extending south to the North Sea and around the British Isles; it has been recorded as far south as Portugal. *Similar Species:* the White-sided Dolphin, which has less white on its sides, a black upper jaw, and a more pointed dorsal fin. Other dolphins have longer beaks.

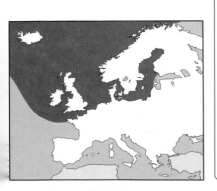

WHITE-BEAKED DOLPHIN

Type	whale
Habitat	marine
Status	not threatened

PHYSICAL DETAILS

Length	up to 3.2m
Weight	up to 275kg
Teeth	<u>22–25</u> 22–25+
Colour	black, grey and white

FOOD AND HABITS

Food	mostly cephalopods, fish
Nest	none
Behaviour	unknown
Voice	unknown
Hibernation	none
Migration	moves south in winter

LIFE CYCLE

Litters	1 every 2–3 years; midsummer
Young	probably 1; active from birth
Maturity	no data
Longevity	no data

Common Porpoise *Phocoena phocoena*

small dorsal fin

blunt head

COMMON PORPOISE

Type	whale
Habitat	coastal marine estuaries
Status	depleted; threatened in many parts of Europe; may be locally extinct

PHYSICAL DETAILS

Length	up to 1.8m
Weight	up to 90kg
Teeth	22–27 / 22–27
Colour	grey above, white below

FOOD AND HABITS

Food	fish; also crustaceans, squid
Nest	none
Behaviour	breathes every 15–20 secs, then dives for 3–6 mins
Voice	echolocation clicks of up to 1000 times per sec
Hibernation	none
Migration	some seasonal movements

LIFE CYCLE

Litters	1 every other year; late summer
Young	1; active from birth
Maturity	females 14 months; males 3 years
Longevity	up to 45 years

One of the most widespread and frequently observed whales in European waters, the Common Porpoise is usually found in coastal waters and estuaries, and often swims up rivers. It has a characteristic movement, rolling forwards to expose the short dorsal fin, but never jumping clear of the water. Common Porpoises are normally gregarious, living in small groups of up to 10, which may coalesce to form larger schools. They have declined dramatically in most parts of their European range due to hunting and drowning in fishing tackle and possibly through poisoning from pesticides. This species is also one of the most commonly stranded.

Range: extends from the Atlantic to the Arctic Ocean; also found in the Baltic, Mediterranean and Black Seas.

Similar Species: none.

Index

Index

Index

Further reading

Ahlen, I., *Identification of Bats in Flight*. (Includes tape of sounds.) SSCN and SYAESC, Stockholm, 1989.

Bang, P., and Dahlstrom, P., *Guide to Animal Tracks and Signs*. Collins, London, 1972.

Corbet, G.B., *The Mammals of the Palaearctic Region*: a Taxonomic Review. British Museum, London, 1978, supplement 1984.

Gorner, M., and Hackethal, H., *Säugetiere Europas*. Neuman, Leipzig, 1988 onwards.

Hutson, A.M., and Greenaway, F., *A Field Guide to British Bats*. Bruce Coleman, London, 1990.

King, J.E., *Seals of the World*. British Musem, Oxford University Press, 1983.

Leatherwood, S., and Reeves, R., *Sierra Club Handbook of Whales and Dolphins*. Sierra Club, San Francisco, 1983.

Lever, C., *Naturalized Mammals of the World*. Longman, London, 1985.

Mitchell-Jones, A.J., et al. *Atlas of European Mammals*. Poyser, London, 1999.

Niethammer, J., and Krapp, F., *Handbuch der Säugetiere Europeas*, Vols 1–6. Aula Verlag, Weisbaden, 1978–

Nowak, R.M., *Walker's Mammals of the World 6th ed.* John Hopkins University Press, Baltimore, 1999.

Parkes, C., and Thornley, J., *Fair Game. The Law of Country Sports and the Protection of Wildlife.* Pelham, London, 1987.

Schober, W., and Grimmberger, E., *A Guide to Bats of Britain and Europe*. Hamlyn, London, 1989.

Watson, L., *A Sea Guide to Whales of the World*. Hutchinson, London, 1981.

Societies and Useful Addresses

Bat Conservation Trust
15 Cloisters House
8 Battersea Park Road
London SW8 4BG
www.bats.org.uk

Biological Records Centre
Monks Wood
Abbotts Ripton
Huntingdon
Cambidgeshire, PE28 2LS
www.brc.ac.uk

Mammal Society
15 Cloisters House
8 Battersea Park Road
London SW8 4BG
www.abdn.ac.uk.mammal

Societas European Mammalogica
Visit their website at *www.european-mammals.org* for comprehensive and up to date information on mammals, and create species lists for any country.

Whale and Dolphin Conservation Society
Alexander House
James Street West
Bath, Avon, BA1 2BT
www.wdcs.org

World Wide Fund for Nature
Panda House
Weyside Park
Godalming
Surrey, GU7 1XR